22
CAREER
BUSTERS

CAREER
BUSTERS

Things People Do to Mess Up

Their Careers and How to Avoid Them

Arthur D. Rosenberg

McGRAW-HILL
New York   San Francisco   Washington, D.C.   Auckland   Bogotá
Caracas   Lisbon   London   Madrid   Mexico City   Milan
Montreal   New Delhi   San Juan   Singapore
Sydney   Tokyo   Toronto

Library of Congress Cataloging-in-Publication Data
Rosenberg, Arthur D.
    Career busters : 22 things people do to mess up their career and
how to avoid them / Arthur D. Rosenberg.
        p.   cm.
    Includes index.
    ISBN 0-07-053991-X (pbk. : alk paper)
    1. Vocational guidance. I. Title.
    HF5381.R7616   1996
    650.1—dc21   96-37269
                                                                   CIP

McGraw-Hill

A Division of The **McGraw·Hill** Companies

1 2 3 4 5 6 7 8 9 0 DOC / DOC 9 0 1 0 9 8 7 6

ISBN 0-07-053991-X

The sponsoring editor for this book was Betsy Brown, the editing supervisor was Fred Dahl, and the production supervisor was Pamela A. Pelton. It was set in Sabon by Inkwell Publishing Services.

Printed and bound by R. R. Donnelley & Sons Company, Inc.

McGraw-Hill books are available at special quantity discounts to use as premiums and sales promotions, or for use in corporate training programs. For more information, please write to the Director of Special Sales, McGraw-Hill, 11 West 19th Street, New York, NY 10011. Or contact your local bookstore.

 This book is printed on recycled, acid-free paper containing a minimum of 50% recycled, de-inked fiber.

To Catherine

▼▼▼

CONTENTS

▼▼

▼▼▼

PREFACE

▼▼▼

> He wins every hand who mingles profit with pleasure, by
> delighting and instructing the reader at the same time.
> —Horace

Some careers blossom, others fade into regret for that which should have been, and a few degenerate into bitterness and resentment. The path to a successful career is strewn with obstacles and dead ends. Successful individuals learn to leap the hurdles, bridge the crevasses, and overcome the many career busters that lie in their way. Smart people learn from their own mistakes, and wise people learn from the experiences of others.

Career busters are obstacles that grow from what we do—or fail to do—and how we do it. External circumstances can damage a profession or an industry, but your career is likely to flourish or flounder as a direct result of your own assets and actions. Other circumstances may cause you inconvenience, but the bottom line of your career is drawn primarily by you.

22 Career Busters takes a problem-solving approach to building and maintaining a successful career. We believe that it is necessary to clearly identify and understand a problem in order to propose a meaningful solution. Our purpose is to identify the most common obstacles to a successful career and to offer strategies for overcoming them.

Each chapter identifies a specific career buster and offers strategies to overcome it. We analyze these problems and potential solutions in a variety of contexts to enable our readers to recognize the obstacles they encounter and to determine the most effective ways to deal with them. Examples, expert opinion, and advice help to put these career busters into perspective and to determine what may be your best approach for your unique set of circumstances. We provide examples, practical advice, and alternatives whenever possible. Understandably, many of our topics are interdependent. For instance, image and communication skills affect your ability to sell yourself and your ideas, exercise control over your environment, become an effective leader, network, or fit into the corporate culture. Nevertheless, we have attempted to present each of these topics as a separate unit within the context of the whole.

In many cases a career buster is a matter of degree: Your interviewing skills or decision-making abilities may be adequate for one position or company, but not quite strong enough for a different environment. Conditions that were never a problem in the past can be particularly difficult to recognize. Also, many positive traits have a negative side. For example, too much self-confidence can be as detrimental as too little, and an excess of control and caution can render you incapable of making important decisions.

Periodically, we need to take reality checks in order to assess our goals and to progress. We need to look as objectively as we can at our successes and our frustrations to seek better ways of doing things. We need to ask ourselves what we are doing wrong, or not doing right, and how we might improve on our performance. Sometimes we need a guide to help us identify and overcome the career busters that are keeping us from getting ahead—like *22 Career Busters*.

To be useful, a career self-help book needs to identify problems that currently or potentially affect *your* career, and to offer practical solutions in a manner and context that *you can actually use*. This includes an awareness of the context in which these circumstances are likely to arise, an understanding of your own tendencies and abilities, and a plan of action based upon realistic alternatives.

This is what *22 Career Busters* offers you: a clear and comprehensive guide to the main obstacles to a successful career, and practical ways to navigate these obstacles successfully. *22 Career Busters* is addressed to people who are already successful and who intend to remain that way, and to those who plan to become successful at whatever career they may choose. This book identifies the most prominent career obstacles and traps, and goes on to reveal how they can be leapt, bridged, or avoided altogether. Our objective is to guide individuals seeking a successful career, as well as corporations striving to open career paths that will attract and keep talented professionals. Our views reflect a thoroughly researched and organized treatment of the issues that affect everyone who is pursuing a career. We've done our best to offer you these ideas and suggestions in a practical context that you can apply to your career and in a writing style we hope you will enjoy reading.

ACKNOWLEDGMENTS

My wife, Catherine, asked me one evening as I was finishing *22 Career Busters,* "When do I get you back?" After more than a year of seeing me working on computer systems during the day and this book during the evenings and weekends, her question made me more fully appreciate her encouragement and her sacrifice.

Thanks go to McGraw-Hill editor Betsy Brown, who proposed the book and waited so patiently for me to complete it; and to Rosalie and Walter Rusak and to Charlie Agius, for their generous and insightful suggestions; and to all the people who agreed to share their thoughts and experiences. I owe a special note of gratitude to my dear friend and alter ego, John Lax, who took me to task, when necessary, and provided a wealth of helpful suggestions.

Arthur D. Rosenberg

22
CAREER
BUSTERS

▼▼▼

CAREER BUSTER 1

IS IMAGE YOUR GREATEST
CAREER OBSTACLE?

Where knowledge and intelligence are born, the great
pretense begins.
—Lao-tzu (from the *Tao Te Ching*)

Self-esteem is how you see yourself; your public image is the way
others see you. Your self- and public images are mirrored re-
flections of each other. Their differences and similarities need to
be understood before either can be managed.

Your vision of yourself is reflected in your interpersonal relationships. It is easier to project a positive public image that is based
upon a sound self-image, and difficult to impress others of what you
yourself are unconvinced. A distorted view of either presents a handicap to both. It is only by understanding the reality of your mirrored
images—personal and public—that you can effectively control them.

This chapter presents the two faces of image: self-esteem and
image control. Its purpose is to encourage you to gain a better understanding and command of each of them and of their interrela-
tionships. We believe that a solid image is the foundation of success
in every aspect of your career, and a launching pad from which to
overcome all of the other career busters.

CAREER SAVERS
Part 1: Self-Image
   The Art of Self-Esteem
Part 2: Public Image
   The Tactics of Image Control

PART 1: SELF-IMAGE

The Art of Self-Esteem

There is no one out there you have to conquer. When you
have successfully conquered yourself, the world will be at
your feet.
—Chin-Ning Chu

1

Once upon a time, according to Hindu legend, all men on earth were gods; but their continuous sins persuaded Brahma to remove the godhead and hide it where it would never be found. One of the gods suggested burying the godhead in the earth; another thought of sinking it in the bottom of the ocean; and a third proposed hiding it high on the tallest mountain. But Brahma rejected these ideas: "Man will learn to dig and dive deep enough, and to climb high enough to find it someday," he said, "so let us hide it where he will never think of looking: within man himself." And so it was.

Self-esteem is the way we think and feel about ourselves. It's an impression based upon respect and liking, the degree to which our egos are satisfied or disappointed, the images we harbor of ourselves. Our inner portrait and the image we project are based upon our understanding and control of these influences. A healthy, balanced ego enables us to get along with ourselves and other people while pursuing our objectives; a distorted or unstable ego is a snake uncaged, as poisonous to the self as it is troublesome to others. The path to self-esteem is a positive self-image based on understanding and acceptance of who and what you are. These are the seeds of growth and confidence, the link between the way you view yourself and how the outside world sees you.

Self-Image

> The good befriend themselves.
> —Sophocles

Self-image is the portrait we construct of ourselves. Your self-image is subjective and unique. You cannot alter the physical reality of your existence—your height and age and history—but you most certainly can modify the way you think and feel about them. If you are not satisfied with the way you see yourself and how the world sees you, change your image!

> Careers are born in kindergarten. Many of them die on the job.

The images we develop of ourselves begin early and evolve into the foundation of our personalities. Positive, negative, and misdirected self-images originate during infancy and are nurtured to maturity. Cultural biases, family influence, economic conditions, and environmental pressures play major roles in our evolving images.

▼▼▼

Back in Clinton, Md., Susan O'Malley's junior high school teacher told her that her dream of becoming the head of a professional sports team was "..not very realistic." (Forbes, March 13, 1995.) But in 1991, at the age of 29, Ms. O'Malley did in fact become the president of the Washington Bullets. Now she's looking for another worthy challenge.

Expectations are programmed into us throughout our childhood. This is when the seeds of anticipation—not just success and failure, but *how much* of each we should expect—are sown. Some people seem to know that they are destined for excellence in whatever they may choose, while others develop doubts as to their ability and, perhaps, their worthiness to succeed. If you expect to win, your chances of success are enhanced; and the expectation of losing makes that a probability.

Self-Understanding

> He who knows others is wise; he who knows himself is enlightened.
> —Lao-tzu

Your perspective of your personality, character, and abilities is acquired over time. Believing in yourself encourages you to expand your goals and provides the energy and confidence to pursue them. However, it is helpful to objectively assess your strengths and weaknesses in order to discover which areas need to be strengthened and which directions may offer the most promise. An exaggerated or distorted view of your skills and talents may persuade you to take foolish and unnecessary risks, while a perceived deficit can limit your expectations and deter you from achieving your potential.

To verify the accuracy of what you think you know about yourself, first look at your track record. Do your friends and colleagues tend to treat you the way you believe that you deserve to be treated? Do most of them appear to appreciate your company and contributions? If not, then there may be a gap between your self- and public images. Next, solicit the opinions of some trusted colleagues and friends. List what you consider to be your major positive and negative qualities in two columns. Support each item with examples and references.

Example:

POSITIVE	NEGATIVE	EXAMPLES	REFERENCES
good listener		People seem to like talking to me.	Betty: Says I'm average. Phil: Says I could be better.
	slow learner	Still not comfortable with computers.	Betty: Disagrees—I learn quickly when I pay attention. Larry: I seem to be better at management and negotiation issues than technical things. Felicia: I'm a quick read with people.
good presentation skills		My last three presentations were well-received.	Betty: Agrees. Phil: O.K., but I sometimes talk too fast. Mack: Same as Phil.
	not considered management material	Haven't been promoted past the lowest management level.	Betty: Keep working at it. Larry: Do I really want to be a manager? Phil: Need to sharpen my image.

This exercise can contribute toward a more accurate assessment of your opinions of yourself and shed some light on the way others see you.

It's natural to critique yourself as long as your criticisms are reasonable and fair. However, introspection should be oriented in the same manner as other forms of appraisal: toward correction and improvement, not punishment. Strive to be as understanding and supportive of yourself as you would be of someone else.

Our ability to evaluate information and make sound decisions is influenced by our moods: A toothache makes the world a dreary place, just as a smiling face can elevate our spirits. That's why things are so much clearer in retrospect, for hindsight works the same on sunny and rainy days. The facts are no longer colored with idle wishes, suspense, or fear. What's done is etched in recognition.

Self-Confidence

> Your attitude, not your aptitude, will determine your altitude.
> —Zig Zigler

Self-confidence is a belief in your ability to make things turn out right. This is what generates the enthusiasm to accept a challenge and the energy to accomplish it. University of Pennsylvania psychology professor Martin E. P. Seligman reminds us that "Life inflicts the same setbacks and tragedies on optimists as it does on pessimists. The difference is that optimists weather them better than pessimists do."

Our self-esteem is only partially based on our accomplishments and largely upon the image we have formed of ourselves. Some people seem to derive little satisfaction from their achievements. They agonize over errors, are intolerant of what they perceive to be their weaknesses and imperfections, and are unable to accept, appreciate, and reward themselves. To avoid the major obstacles to self-acceptance:

- Don't compare yourself to other people.
- Don't let anybody pull you down.
- Don't wallow in the past.
- Don't accept unhappiness.

Attitudes are tendencies that can be encouraged or changed. Having a positive mental attitude is like being programmed for success, and the opposite is also true. Napoleon Hill, an advisor to Franklin Roosevelt and a close associate of Andrew Carnegie, promoted his concept of PMA (positive mental attitude) as the cornerstone of success. Its purpose is to identify and pursue goals, to form good relationships, and also to enjoy the process. "PMA allows you to build on hope and overcome the negative attitudes of despair and discouragement," he wrote. "It gives you the mental power, the feeling, the confidence to do anything you make up your mind to do."

PART 2: PUBLIC IMAGE

The Tactics of Image Control

> Fame .. is nothing but an empty name.
> —Charles Churchill

Image control is how you represent yourself to the world. It requires recognition of the image you *are* projecting, a clear picture of the image you *would like* to project, and an understanding of how to bring these into harmony.

Public Image. Your public image is your signature to the outside world, a portrait of who and what you are. It influences people toward or away from you on matters such as trust, confidence, and whether they want to be around you. Although based to a large extent on your self-image, your public image is more readily subject to control and modification. But this control is only possible if you have an objective view of the way others see you.

> WABC program director John Mainelli, now in his mid-forties, raised WABC from 30th place to first in the ratings. In the 1960's, he did radio broadcasts for the leftist subculture in San Francisco; today he books former NYC mayor Ed Koch, archconservative Rush Limbaugh (the fellow who refers to feminists as "Feminazis"), and Bob Grant (alias Robert Gigante), who rationalizes his racist remarks with, "Aren't we all in show biz? And isn't hatred the hottest number these days?" When asked whether the programming fits his own convictions, Mainelli smiled incredulously: "Convictions? I don't get paid for that." (Der Spiegel, Hamburg, Germany, 4-3-95.)

Even though you cannot see yourself exactly as others do, you can approximate the exercise by watching how people react to you and by being sensitive to their reactions. Think about the people with whom you often come in contact at work: What do you suppose they think of you? Do they ask for your opinion and pay attention to you when you talk? Is your judgement valued? Are you considered a loyal employee? A team player? A leader? If you're not sure, the simplest way to find out may be to ask a few colleagues whom you respect and trust. If you haven't yet received any direct feedback, you may have a misconception about the way you are perceived.

Interpersonal Style

Your style is the projection of your preferred image.

Interpersonal style is how we deal with other people. It is the foundation of the image we portray to those with whom we come in contact. Style is how we control our relationships with people and let them know who and what we are. The personal style you choose to exhibit depends upon the purpose you are trying to achieve and how your style compares to that of the other person. Do you want to be noticed or ignored? Do you wish to provoke a response or calm things down? Are you giving orders, making suggestions, or asking for assistance? Do you want obedience, cooperation, respect, or only to avoid confrontation?

Actor Peter Falk's well-known character, Columbo, portrays himself as a seemingly clumsy and inept police detective in a frumpy raincoat. His appearance and low-key manner tend to disarm his adversaries, usually men and women of some prominence. Columbo's purpose is to apprehend the villains, not to convince them of his competence, of which the viewing audience is already aware. His self-effacing style is used to lure the guilty into revealing more than they intend. It is only at the end, when it is too late for caution, that they perceive the detective's keenly analytical mind.

What is the nature of your relationship with the other person: Boss or staff? Colleague, acquaintance, or stranger? Are you friendly, hostile, or indifferent to one another? Is there an existing image to be maintained or changed? Effective image control relies on a clear assessment of your personal style and that of your target audience. Although few people fit neatly into clearly defined types, tendencies and patterns do emerge, and it can be useful to recognize them and understand what to expect from them.

Type 1. Confident, brash, and intimidating; intent on getting where he's going.

Type 2. Verbose, sociable, and analytical; likes discussions and debates.

Type 3. Quiet and evasive, easily intimidated; avoids taking a firm position.

Types 1 & 2. Direct, verbose, enthusiastic, intense; can be self-righteous and overwhelming.

Types 2 & 3. Good talker and listener; warm, pleasant, and patient; likes to discuss problems; can be intimidated.

Alternating. Adaptable; thinks things through before deciding which style is appropriate; hard to predict.

Projecting Your Image

> It is better to be beautiful than good.
> But it is better to be good than ugly.
> —Oscar Wilde

Before attempting to project your image to the world, take a little time to observe the players and their styles. What might be the best way of getting through to them? Often, the most effective way of making a positive impression on others is to match or complement their style as best you can. Remember that your value to people is an image based on their perception of your utility to them.

> It used to be who you know; today, it's more a matter of
> how well you get along with them.
> —Ruhtra

The qualities that help us get along with people over a period of time can be difficult to assess during an initial meeting. Stability, reliability, integrity, accomplishment, and consideration for other people are among the personal qualities that people most admire. In our fast-paced society, however, we don't always have enough time to really get to know everyone we encounter, so we often resort to outward symbols of these virtues. This is why it's so important to be conscious of the impressions we are making on people, and how they are responding to us.

> Early impressions are hard to eradicate from the mind.
> —Saint Jerome

A friend raised in Taiwan told us, "I was taught as a child always to hand things to an adult with two hands. This simple habit made a good impression on my teachers in grade school. They told me that I had good people skills and leadership qualities, which encouraged me to assume responsibilities. The impression must have rubbed off on me, because I grew up full of confidence."

Everyone is influenced by first impressions; many of us give an exaggerated importance to our initial judgments and are unwilling to change our minds later on. Open-minded people may be less emphatic and more willing to modify their opinions, but it is difficult even for them to completely overcome their earliest impressions. Clearly, first impressions bear an influence on future relationships, and so they need to be controlled.

When forming an impression of someone else, try to reserve your own judgment as long as possible. Resist making up your mind until you've had a chance to observe him or her. Think about the checklist you use to project your image: How well is the other person following these guidelines? Does she appear natural and at ease? Does he seem sincere? Make a written or mental note of the characteristics that impress you, and consider incorporating them into your personal repertoire. Note also the behaviors that trouble or annoy you, and ask yourself if you are guilty of any of these. Use the opportunity of meeting new people not only to form impressions of them, but also to improve your own impression-making skills.

You can't totally control what other people think of you, but you most certainly can influence their impression by managing your behavior. Learning to control your public image really isn't all that difficult once you get the hang of it, and the effort is more than reimbursed by the reward. *What* impression you wish to create is up to you; our objective here is to help you to control the image you want to project, beginning with the first impressions that you make on other people.

In our experience, the best way to create a good impression is to dress appropriately for the occasion and the impression you wish to make; smile, shake hands firmly, and:

—*be pleasant:* you only get one chance to make a first impression;

—*be calm and composed:* avoid displaying any nervousness or anxiety;

—*be courteous:* rudeness is one of the strongest barriers to human relations;

—*be attentive:* allow others to reveal as much of themselves as they will;

—*be patient:* no one actually dies of boredom;

—*be upbeat:* try to save your negative comments until after the initial meeting;

—*be prepared:* if you have an agenda, be ready to support it;

—*be consistent:* never contradict yourself or your position;

—*be alert:* don't let yourself be baited or sidetracked;

—*be aware:* notice how others are reacting to you;

—*be controlled:* do what you set out to do, or change your plan as needed;

—*be flexible:* look for an alternative plan or course of action;

—*be yourself:* false impressions are impossible to live up to.

Many of these suggestions are just common sense, but we use them as a checklist to remind us of our purpose.

> Praise nauseates me, but woe betide the person who
> doesn't recognize my worth.
> —(former UN Secretary General) Dag Hammarskjold

If your plan or action does not enlist support on its own merit, then the approval you seek must depend on other considerations. This is a common reality in business and social activities, where politics and personal agendas are pursued along with common purpose. However, seeking approval for yourself—the inner person—is often seen as a flag of uncertainty and insecurity. When you query colleagues, do you ask them what they think, or only if they agree with you? And when someone criticizes or disagrees with you, do you defend yourself or just listen?

There is a subtle distinction between seeking approval and soliciting honest feedback. The difference is less in *how* you ask than *why*—to reinforce your position or to obtain other opinions and perspectives; to gain reassurance or to gather information. Often the only way to tell is by how closely someone listens to unflattering replies.

Making Adjustments

> Do unto others as they would like.

If you are having trouble getting along with someone, observe the person's mode of talking and behavior: Is she quiet and reserved, or friendly and gregarious? Focused on results, or detail oriented? Is your style quite different from his? Would you like to improve the relationship? You may be able to do just that by altering the way you deal with that person.

Adjusting to someone else's style is an attempt to get along better. Extreme differences may require patience and a little flexibility, but the results can be dramatic. Subtle variations are more difficult to identify but easier to accommodate. The people with whom you get along most easily, and those whose styles you find most difficult to pin down, may be accommodating you.

> Employee: *I want to succeed in the worst way.*
> Boss: *Well, you're right on track!*

Tact is knowing how to handle difficult and delicate situations without offending people. Tactful people are sensitive, considerate, and diplomatic; tactless types are crude, vulgar, and indiscreet. The key to being tactful is to be aware of people's circumstances and considerate of their feelings. The value is in making people more receptive to you without aggravating their discomfort. Tactlessness may be couched in humor (can't you take a little joke?) bordering on malice. It can also stem from ignorance (what I don't know about you doesn't hurt me) and indifference (hey, I've got my own problems). The trouble with these approaches—aside from hurting people—is that they will cause most people to avoid contact with you whenever possible.

Presence

> You can make more friends in two months by becoming interested in other people than you can in two years by trying to get people interested in you.
> —Dale Carnegie

Your public image is influenced by the way you look and sound to those around you. Are you noticed when you enter a room? Do you want others to notice you? What impression do you make on people who meet you for the first time? Are you comfortable with the way people react to you?

Presence is an aura that lets people know you're to be reckoned with. We're not talking about flamboyance or artificial attention-getting showmanship, but an air of confidence and readiness for whatever may occur. Watch successful individuals when they appear at meetings and other get-togethers: They smile, shake hands enthusiastically, and refer to people by name. They make meaningful eye contact and pay attention to what is said to them. They are polite, purposeful, and composed.

The way you dress, groom, and carry yourself are the main contributing factors to your appearance. A calm, relaxed manner, smooth and confident movements, and good posture contribute to a positive impression. Think of this as packaging the product that you represent.

> The eyes believe themselves; the ears believe other people.
> —German proverb

Eye contact is an effective way of letting people know who you are, a powerful influence, and a form of unspoken intimacy. Confident individuals make eye contact and are slow to break it. And they are quick to smile, another sign of confidence and control. The handshaking ritual is the primary form of physical contact between people in a work environment. We recommend the firm and friendly handshake—one of the worst impressions people make is by offering a limp hand. The length of a handshake can impart special meaning:

very brief shows limited interest; firm and held for four or five seconds suggests enthusiasm; longer than that may be suggestive and inappropriate.

> Fish die by their mouth.
> —Japanese proverb

Voice is second only to physical appearance as an image-builder or deflator. A clear, confident, and pleasant voice will enhance your image just as surely as a nervous, stuttering, inaudible, squeaky, or somehow unpleasant pattern of speech can damage it. Beware as well of poor grammar and inappropriate language. If you have reason to suspect a problem in this area, verify it with a few trusted friends and seek professional instruction.

Image Control. Image isn't everything, but a poor self- or public image can undermine an otherwise promising career. Successful people have learned that their self-image, and the image they project to others, are subject to a good deal of their own control. Initially, image control can be hard work; eventually it becomes a habit, as natural as a smile.

▼▼▼

CAREER BUSTER 2

IF YOU FAIL TO COMMUNICATE
YOU HAVEN'T GOT A PRAYER

No one can read your mind, fortunately.

In school, English was viewed as little more than a subject to be factored into one's grade average—for some, an ordeal to survive and hopefully forget forever. Few of us recognized it as a tool with which to shape our future careers. Later on, we may resort to rationalizing our poor and deteriorating communication skills by convincing ourselves that we don't really need them.

Similarly with writing, we jot barely literate notes on memo pads, post-its, or electronic mail when necessary and hire specialists to write the manuals and proposals that cannot be avoided. How frustrating it can be to make ourselves understood, win our share of arguments, or convince those around us of our point of view! But for those who know how to communicate effectively—to get their messages across to others with a minimum of confusion and misunderstanding—this very same world behaves more reasonably.

CAREER SAVERS

The Art of Effective Communication
The Tactics of Effective Communication
Oral Tactics
Written Tactics

The Art of Effective Communication

> Sixty percent of all management problems result from
> faulty communications.
> —Peter Drucker

Communication skills are among the most important assets of a successful careerperson. Whether you want to share an idea, obtain information, persuade someone to accept your agenda, or merely socialize, you must communicate effectively to be successful. Everyone communicates, more or less, but there is an important difference between truly effective, barely adequate, and inept communication. Superior communicators get more attention than their counterparts; often, they receive more credit for their accomplishments and the lion's share of raises and promotions. In contrast, poor communicators are confused, frustrated, and resentful when their contributions are undervalued and they themselves go relatively unnoticed.

To improve your communication skills:

1. *Assess your major weaknesses.*
Do your best to obtain honest feedback from friends, family members, and trusted colleagues to identify your major weaknesses. When someone is willing to offer an opinion, write it down and thank them, no matter how much you may disagree. Don't argue or protest that they don't understand, or they are unlikely to be frank with you the next time around. Review your notes at a later, quiet time. If several people mention the same point, there is probably some truth to it; and even if an issue is raised only once, it may be worth thinking about.

2. *Form a plan of action.*
Having identified or confirmed your major communication problems, set about to solve them with professional guidance. Most neighborhoods and communities offer many types of communication classes through local colleges, civic and religious groups, and other organizations. Books and self-help courses are excellent ways to supplement and reinforce your plans. Of course, learning new tricks and changing old habits is hard work, but the reward is an improved ability to present yourself to the world, and better career options.

▪ *A Special Note to the Non-Native English Speaker*
If your native language is not English, you may fall into the enormous group of people who are frustrated by the difficulty of having to communicate professionally in a "foreign" tongue. Realistically, only the most gifted linguists ever learn to speak and write a second language like a native, unless they begin as children. Many former professionals have to settle for menial jobs, with little hope of being promoted to upper management positions, because of language difficulties.

The solution is to make the effort to improve your verbal skills by taking classes and practicing with people who are willing to correct you. Bear in mind that even people who recognize and respect your other skills and talents may avoid working with you because of the effort they must make to understand you, and management may be reluctant to entrust you with the responsibilities that could enrich your career.

The Tactics of Effective Communication

> You can have brilliant ideas, but if you can't get them across, your ideas won't get you anywhere.
> —Lee Iacocca

There are tactics, such as timing and use of supportive data and leverage, that are common to both speaking and writing. Others apply exclusively to one or the other: Body language and tone of voice can only be used in face-to-face conversation, while permanent records and signed agreements are limited to the written realm. Let's take a look at the common tactics and how they are applied.

Defining Your Objective

> Hold thou the good; define it well.
> —Alfred, Lord Tennyson

The single most important aspect of effective communication is the one most often ignored—the purpose. Without a clear goal, the potential success of a discussion, memo, or report is left to the hazard of the wind. This issue is so important that we'll return to it within the contexts of both verbal and written tactics.

Qualifying Your Objective. The second most important question is the ability and willingness of the person with whom you are communicating to contribute toward your objective. Is he a decision maker, or able to influence a decision maker? *(If not, why are you addressing him?)* Is she inclined to agree or disagree with your position? *(Have you done your homework?)* Is he willing to assist or cooperate with you? *(What's in it for him?)* Are you presenting your argument in the manner that she is most likely to understand and accept? *(More homework!)* Suppose someone is too busy or uninterested to award you the attention you would like. You might:

1. *Prepare a presentation that will appeal to them.* Seek an issue of particular interest to your audience and use it to make your own communication appealing. Keep it focused and succinct.

2. *Address yourself to someone else.* Is there an alternate audience who might be more sympathetic to your cause? What do you gain or lose by shifting gears? Can you leverage a secondary audience to influence the primary target?

3. *Don't bother.* Is this communication necessary? Might you have more to lose than gain with it?

To get someone to see things your way, it is useful to first understand how they see things their way. It's difficult to get somewhere until you know where somewhere is. The manner in which you present your point of view can be as important as the substance. It is a reality of life that people tend to see things from their own unique perspective, and it is unrealistic to expect them to automatically acknowledge yours. Presenting your version of reality—the truth as you see it—is an art form that displays your view in its most favorable light. This often means emphasizing the positive aspects of your idea while de-emphasizing the negative. It may mean selectively including or omitting certain details, and clarifying some of these details while shrouding others in ambiguity. It is likely to require careful timing and corroboration, e.g., documents, statistics, and leverage.

Timing

> Time is that wherein there is opportunity ...
> —Hippocrates

Knowing when to suggest, request, or counter someone else's initiative can enhance your chances for success. Windows of opportunity open and close like rays of sunshine peeking through the clouds, and you need to be sensitive to the timetables of (1) your target and (2) the circumstances affecting your objective. Asking for a signature on Friday afternoon, when your busy boss is trying to wrap things up for the weekend, may result in immediate action; or is he likely to desk it until the following Monday? Lining up early allies for your objective may lock it in and leverage valuable support; or will the enthusiasm ebb as time passes without activity? Setting realistic deadlines and meeting them builds credibility; missed deadlines reflect negatively on you and your agenda. Acting at the wrong time can alienate potential allies, while failing to act may leave you out in the cold. (See Chapter 14.)

Supportive Corroboration. Impressive numbers and statistics, examples, attachments, and leverage are among the tools of support in proving the importance, relevance, and accuracy of your plan. If money (revenues/expenses) is the issue, favorable comparisons may help to establish your point:

> Since sales are up by 7%, we feel that an increase in advertising of only 3.8% is justified to maintain our positive momentum.
> Our ratio of representatives to revenue is 1:$557K as compared to an industry average of 1:$482K.

Select your distribution list—those to whom you choose to send or not send copies of your correspondence—carefully.

Oral Tactics

> One ought, every day at least, .. if it were possible, to speak a few reasonable words.
> —Johann Wolfgang von Goethe

Select the most advantageous means of communicating with your target audience. If they are located in another location, you may be limited to the phone or written media. If they are within visual range, remember to put your best face forward. People remember little courtesies and kindnesses. Do you listen to what others tell you, or do you interrupt them with stories of your own? Do you ask, "How are you today?" and keep on walking before you've heard an answer? Do you refer back to something someone said earlier ("Has your daughter made a decision about college?")? Do you follow up on promises? Do you show appreciation for favors done for you? Do you have a goal, and are you doing what is needed to accomplish it?

Face-to-Face

> Seek first to understand, then to be understood.

Communicating successfully generally hinges on your ability to listen. Certainly good speaking patterns and body language are part of the process, but listening skills are what separate the winners from the pack. The different *types of listening* can be broken down into three levels:

Level 1: *Perfunctory listening.* Perfunctory (superficial) listening is similar to watching television while reading a newspaper: You can hear what the speaker is saying, but you're paying only selective attention, if that. This is insulting and, of course, ineffective listening.

Level 2: *Listening to respond.* Most of us listen primarily with the purpose of responding. This causes us to apply what we hear to our own values and interests, and thus to miss at least some of the speaker's reasons and intentions. This can help to answer questions and win arguments, but it can also lead to confusion.

Level 3: *Listening to understand.* Listening to understand what someone wants to say requires empathy and patience. Empathetic listening means trying to put yourself in the other person's place in order to see things from their point of view. Patience means giving them the chance to express themselves fully, without causing them to rush or stop. The reward for your effort is accuracy of understanding and, more often than not, gaining the confidence and trust of the speaker.

Body Language.   Body language represents about 60% of the communication process, with perhaps 30% dependent on the sounds we make, and only 10% left to our words. Body language is expressed by two distinctive areas of anatomy: above the neck and below the neck.

1. *Above the neck.* The way (and timing with which) you direct your eyes, tilt your head, and stretch your lips constitutes the majority of your unspoken language. In face-to-face communication, the eyes possess the loudest voice. A raised eyebrow in greeting acknowledges another person; the same gesture while they're speaking may signal surprise or skepticism. Refusal to raise the eyebrow can be a sign of disapproval (or poor eyesight). Nervous gestures and darting eyes evoke distrust.

   During a conversation, the direction in which you look speaks volumes:

   —Looking *straight* at the other person means they have your attention; a prolonged stare, especially when the other person isn't talking, can be used to signal disapproval, anger, or (accompanied with a smile) a desire for greater intimacy.

—Looking *downward* is an invitation for the other person to speak.

—Looking *sideways* signals a lack of interest and may make the other person uncomfortable.

—Looking *upward* can be a pause, as when you're searching for a word and would prefer not to be interrupted—or it may confuse and disorient the listener.

2. *Below the neck.* Body stance varies between men and women and groups of different geographic origins. Many women tend to face the person to whom they're speaking straight on, while a man often prefers a slightly side-on stance.

Telephone Conversations. On the phone, it is especially important to speak in a clear, well-paced voice, neither so quickly as to challenge the other person's understanding nor so slowly as to strain their patience. Impatience, annoyance, and anger are easily conveyed by phone; and they can also be more easily concealed. Remember as well to pronounce your name and number clearly when you leave them on an answering machine—it is very frustrating to receive a mumbled message.

Written Tactics

Written communication consists for the most part of memos, letters, reports, and proposals. Within the business environment, letters can be grouped with memos, and we shall take the liberty of treating reports together with proposals. Bear in mind that anything you write, sign, and send can be shown to others, and filed for future use.

The effectiveness of your written communication depends upon the manner in which it is received. Be sure to support your arguments, and follow up to assure that your message has been recognized and understood. When you write, your specific objective is usually to *respond, initiate,* or *record.*

Providing information can be a straightforward process. Make sure you understand precisely what is being asked (and by whom), and that your data are accurate.

> The best argument is that which seems merely an explanation.
> —Dale Carnegie

Defending yourself is a complicated and vital art. The essentials are to differentiate between an attack that needs a written defense and one that does not, and among attacks against yourself, your position, or your ideas. There are many books that deal specifically with these issues. Defensive and offensive techniques are discussed in depth in another of our books, *Manipulative Memos*.

When you initiate a communiqué, your objective and your message should be clear. Ask yourself what you are trying to accomplish when you begin, how you plan to accomplish it while you are writing, and whether you have accomplished it when you are finished. The general rules are:

1. If it isn't necessary, don't write it.

2. If you have a point to make, support it.

3. Reveal only what you want the reader to know.

4. Consider what you have to lose as well as gain by sending it.

5. Make sure it's understandable (unless you want it to be ambiguous).

6. Make it error free: if possible, have someone you trust read it.

7. Follow up as needed.

An example of #5 was FBI Chief J. Edgar Hoover's reaction to the reduced size of his new memo sheets (intended to cut costs). "Watch the borders," Hoover impatiently scrawled along the margin. And for several weeks afterward, incoming road traffic from Canada and Mexico was exceptionally slow.

Everyone likes to be appreciated. The simple act of sending a thank-you note to acknowledge someone's help, no matter how small or insignificant, is likely to incline that person to respond with favor to a future request from you. Clever executives, managers, and secretaries have been using this effective tactic with enormous success for years.

▼▼▼

CAREER BUSTER 3

YOU CAN'T PROMOTE A PRODUCT OR A SERVICE IF YOU CAN'T SELL YOURSELF

> When you market yourself, you get to keep your most valuable asset.

Nearly everybody sells. We promote our images of what should or should not be, of what we wish to be allowed to do, of what we'd like to happen. We sell our ideas, and we do this by marketing ourselves. We sell when we interview for a job, seek a raise or advancement, submit a proposal, manage a project, negotiate a deal, or pursue a goal that requires someone else's approval.

The purpose of this chapter is to emphasize the role of this undervalued element in building a successful career, and to reveal some of its basic strategies. This is not a primer for aspiring marketing professionals. Our goal is to borrow from the "tricks of the trade" and help you apply them to *your* career. Think of them as tools in selling the most important product in the history of the world: you.

CAREER SAVERS
The Art of Selling
The Tactics of Selling

The Art of Selling

> Selling is the art of gaining acceptance.

Wil Larsson is a successful career salesman from Oregon now living in the state of Washington. Wil writes, "It was a cold, windy, and rain-soaked day in Portland, Oregon, when I finally graduated from college after five years of struggling to keep dry. I took an offer with a big corporation in sales. They moved me to San Francisco for training and then to Los Angeles—the fast track!

"I thought I had to ..you know ..'sell' people things they didn't want or couldn't use. The *presentation* was the key; once I mastered the presentation, I had the steps-of-the-sale wired: introduction (name, company, product); social period (weather, family, sports); transition to the presentation (subtly getting to the point); presentation (brochure, catalogue, samples, charts); features and benefits (profits, costs, quality, competitive advantages); summary (why buy); close (let's write up the sale); shut up (stoic silence); answer questions (overcome objections); write order (finally); thank customer for order (I feel good/you feel good).

"I spent a lot of the company's money making presentations ..I was, in fact, in the presentation business. Unfortunately, I wasn't selling a lot of widgets. It wasn't long before I began to lose faith in myself as a salesperson. Alternatively I blamed the company. It wasn't ..couldn't be *me*, it had to be the crummy products that wouldn't sell. After all, the presentation was perfect, wasn't it? This string of logic was confounded only by the minor detail that *other* salespeople *were* selling the products. A year later I was still in trouble. Then something happened—I began to observe how other salespeople tried to sell me when I went out to buy something or other. Some of them were good, while others turned me off. A modest investment of attention and reflection led me to the conclusion that the ones I liked were those who seemed to know what I wanted. They didn't talk a whole lot, but when they did, I was glad to listen. That's because they focused on the things in which I was interested. How did they know?

"The answer was a revelation that altered my entire attitude toward selling: The best salespeople knew what I wanted because they were listening to me and crafting their presentation to blend with my own wants and needs. My clear objective from that time on was to listen and only present when appropriate. Lead the customer by asking questions about what he or she would like to own. Operate as if the customer was paying me for advice on purchasing the perfect product or service. My goal was then and thereafter to serve, and the way to serve was through careful listening."

The Tactics of Selling

Stepping to their side gives you the inside track.

Tactics are the steps that lead to a desirable conclusion. The steps in our simplified version of successful selling are getting in the door, making your pitch, overcoming objections, and closing the sale. These tactics apply not only to salespeople, but to everyone who has occasion to interview for a job, seek a promotion or salary increase, support a project in which they have a vested interest, or negotiate a deal.

Getting Their Attention

It pays to advertise.

One of the most popular stories told at sales conventions is the one about the handyman who ran the following ad in a local newspaper: *I can fix whatever your husband can fix, and I can do it now!* Of course, once he got in the door he had to deliver on his promise. But first, he had to get in.

Making the Presentation

..to convince is to weaken.
—Sidonie Gabrielle Colette

Wil Larsson's presentation list is representative of the tactics used by the pro's in a variety of industries: introduction, small talk, and the rest. Many of these same principles, applied with flexibility and imagination, can be used to sell your personal agenda. The key here is to convince your prospect that your objective also serves their interests, or at least that it does not conflict with theirs. This means packaging your proposal so as to make it appear advantageous to (1) the company, (2) the decision maker, or (3) preferably both. Look at it from their perspective: Why should they take a chance on you if they see nothing to be gained for them? Would you do the same for someone else? Have you? Just because you believe that your request is fair doesn't guarantee that others share your view. They have their own agendas and priorities. Unless you link your plan to the interests of your prospects, they may not buy it.

> Retired executive Walter R. tells of the salesman who oversold himself. "Some years ago a salesman would call on me arriving in a Caddy and wearing a $300 suit (a Lexus and a Gucci might be today's equivalents). We would go to lunch at Sid Allen's (five-star restaurant). He was selling paper boxes at about 5 cents each. He never made a sale to me ..you can probably guess why."

Meeting Their Needs.   It's easier to sell someone what they *want* than what they *need*. Needs are met by recognizing or creating another person's comfort zone and satisfying it. This can be done in a positive or negative manner. The positive approach is generally preferred, as it promotes a more agreeable atmosphere: *Here are the advantages of doing what I want you to do.* When this proves ineffective, the negative tack may be worth the risk: *This is what will/may happen if you don't do what I want.* The problem with using negatives is that your target may decide to call your bluff.

People tend to take notice of the following positive/negative pairs of words: increase/decrease; improve/worsen; gain/loss; save/cost; new/old; sooner/later.

Positive Examples:

1. Doing this will lead to an increase in production.
2. If you buy this, it will improve the quality of that.
3. This will save you $$ over a period of six months.

Negative Examples:

1. Not doing this will lead to a decrease in production.
2. If you don't buy this, the quality of that will decrease.
3. That will cost you $$ over a period of six months.

Negotiating

> The single most important skill in negotiation is the ability to put yourself in the other side's shoes.
> —William Ury

The importance of being able to see an issue from another point of view keeps coming up throughout this and other chapters in *22 Career Busters.* That's because it is essential to every level of human interaction in which a person wants to win someone else's agreement or approval. In this section, we add a third perspective, that of a neutral party with nothing to gain or lose.

Our basic strategy is to (1) identify the major points of agreement and disagreement between their view and ours, (2) discover the reason for their disagreement (i.e., the "problem"), (3) seek a solution to the problem, (4) explore a common ground between their view and ours that is acceptable to both of us, and (5) try to create a win/win situation from which we both benefit.

From the other person's perspective, try to:

1. Understand how they see the issue.
2. Identify the reasons for their differing views, e.g., constraints, risks, fears.

—Use empathetic listening (Chapter 2) to encourage them to speak openly.

—Focus on their perceptions, not on yours.

—Acknowledge their perspective by addressing it and by demonstrating understanding and respect.

3. Seek to resolve the cause of their objection, not to argue it away.

From the neutral perspective:

1. Identify the similiarities and differences between your view and theirs.

2. Use the common points to create an aura of agreement.

3. Re-evaluate your own position in light of what you've learned.

4. Focus on resolving the differences without taking sides.

To summarize, the successful negotiator is called upon to define areas of mutual agreement and to overcome objections. The most effective way to influence a negotiation is by understanding *why* people believe and behave as they do, and by addressing their concerns.

Overcoming Objections

> Being subject to influence is the key to influencing others.

Getting past *no* means dealing effectively with objections. It begins with realizing that the vast majority of *no's* don't mean "not ever," but rather "I'm not completely sure yet," or "I'm not ready to make a decision." The message to be derived from this is that if you give up at the first sign of refusal (as many people do), you won't get what you want. If you persist, your chances of succeeding are likely to increase. Of course, there are situations where insisting will not work, and you need to be sensitive to people's reactions and the circumstances that influence their decisions. Nevertheless, it helps to know how to overcome a negative response in situations where a little effort may turn the tide in your favor.

Sales training courses categorize the types of knowledge needed to surmount the customer's objections. For our purposes, we offer the four rules of persistence:

1. *Maintain a positive attitude.* Always expect to succeed. Treat *no* as an unexpected surprise that doesn't mean "never," but just "not yet." Promote your case in an enthusiastic manner.

2. *Be reasonable.* Focus your efforts on what is realistically attainable. Recognize when to back off, when to regroup, and when to persist.

3. *Be prepared.* Do your homework: Research and weigh the political, financial, and personal factors that are likely to influence the decision or result you are seeking. Have the data ready to justify your proposal, and be prepared to sell it to your target.

4. *Consider the other person's point of view.* If a favorable decision depends on convincing other people, try to see things from their side. If you were in their place, how would you react? Does your petition coincide with their interests? Can you state your objective in a way that might be more meaningful to them?

Closing.   Professional salespeople tell us that *closing* is the single most important tactic in successful selling. It is also a vital part of winning agreement for a raise, promotion, or proposal. In sales, closing is the way you help the customer to decide to buy. On a broader perspective, closing is how you assist your target to agree to your request.

Example 1: Sales
>The professional salesperson moves to close the sale.
>
>Seller: *Do you like the product?*
>
>Customer: *Well, yes, it seems to meet our needs.*
>
>Seller: *Great. In what quantity can we write up the sale?*
>
>From this point on, the first person to speak buys the product (/service):
>
>—if the customer speaks first, he buys the product (the sale is made);
>
>—if the salesperson speaks first, he buys it back (i.e., loses the sale).

Example 2: Everyday Situations
>You: *Do you agree that (it) is justified?*
>
>Target: *Well, yes, it seems reasonable.*
>
>You: *Thank you. Will you approve it?*
>
>Remember to thank the decision maker for approving your request.

Why is closing necessary? Because experience shows that most customers will not buy unless you specifically ask for their business. In fact, 80% of customers expect to be asked for the sale, according to a study conducted by the (British) Institute of Purchasing Management. Similarly, your request is less likely to be forgotten, shelved, or turned down once you get the other party to commit.

CAREER BUSTER 4

IF YOU ARE AN INEFFECTIVE LEADER, YOU WILL NOT BE FOLLOWED

Manage things and lead people.

A good leader understands the difference between leadership and management; a poor leader fails to make this elementary distinction. You can manage time, financial resources, production, inventory, conflict, and other *things.* If you try to manage people, you will fail as a leader.

Classical Western management concepts are neatly encapsulated in the cliché, "We can't all be winners." In an environment where this is true, it follows that there must be losers. Dr. W. Edwards Deming believed this to be the focal point of what is wrong with Western thinking as embodied by our stagnant MBO (management by objectives) and other unproductive theories. Some corporations, like Ford, IBM, AT&T, Burlington Industries, and Procter & Gamble, are beginning to reverse this trend, but others have yet to catch on. Why do so many companies continue to pursue philosophies that have dead-ended into a staggering deficit? There are probably three main reasons:

1. *Momentum. If it ain't broke, don't fix it.*
   It is difficult to change direction once a habit pattern has been formed.
2. *Vested interest. We got where we are doing things our way.*
   People who have risen to prominence are often reluctant to alter the patterns that got them there.
3. *Ingenuity: If it's broke, fix it.*
   We invent clever patches and improvements to help plug the leaks.

CAREER SAVERS
The Art of Leadership
The Tactics of Leadership

▼▼▼

The Art of Leadership

> Leadership is getting others to share the dirty work.

Good leadership maximizes human effort. A leader is a teacher who enhances the skills and energy of others while directing them toward a goal. The most effective way to lead is by example—even those who hardly listen to a word you say observe a good deal more of what you do.

Leadership vs Management

> Management is doing things right; leadership is doing the right things.
> —Warren Bennis and Peter Drucker

The differences and the relationship between these parallel concepts are the keys to understanding what it means to be a leader. The leader is the one who creates priorities and decides what to do first; the manager then creates the schedule and the plan to make it happen. In other words, the leader determines what should be accomplished, and then the manager figures out how to do it. This distinction is often blurred, for managers may need to both manage (things) and lead (people) to be successful.

Suppose, for example, that a company decides to manufacture widgets. Corporate leadership (Board of Directors, CEO, CFO, etc.) makes the strategic decisions, e.g., to invest $12 million to produce 300,000 widgets at $40 each. Management then steps in to make the tactical decisions as to where the factory should be located, the necessary amount of automation and labor, and so on.

Middle management has the responsibility of running the daily operation of the factory, like seeing to it that quality and production standards are met, controlling costs, etc. Most managers who supervise or work closely with other workers also have a leadership role to fill; this takes the form of observing, listening, resolving, motivating, and teaching.

Leadership vs Supervision

> The boss says, "Go!"; the leader, "Let's go!"
> —Harry Gordon Selfridge

Nor is leadership the same as supervision. Traditional supervision is embodied by the line manager who usually has a good deal of hands-on experience.

We read about a poultry plant where production had fallen behind schedule. Management warned the supervising staff that heads would roll if chickens weren't cleaned and packaged much more quickly. The supervisors, who had no training in leadership, passed the word down to the workers, cautioning them to waste less time socializing and to focus on their tasks. The workers, fearful for their jobs, indeed began to work more quickly, sacrificing safety and quality for speed. Initially, production increased, and for a while the management was happy. However, several other things occurred to mitigate their pleasure:

1. Accidents accelerated: Workers were cutting their hands and fingers more often and more seriously than ever before. [*Sick leave and turnovers increased.*]

2. Waste escalated: Good portions of the chickens were being sliced away with the unusable parts. [*Costs began to rise and profits fell.*]

3. Quality decreased: More inedible parts and contaminants were finding their way into the packages. [*Customers complained and sales declined.*]

Management rushed forth to find out what was wrong. The supervisors and workers deemed responsible were fired, and the rest were warned to turn things around if they wanted to keep their jobs. Unfortunately, nobody explained to the supervisors and workers precisely which things were to be turned around, or how. Conditions grew worse, leading to more firings and defections. Management decided to cut their losses and sold the plant to the highest bidder.

The new owner knew more about management than chickens. She visited the plant personally and talked to the remaining staff. She asked about the things she didn't know and took careful notes. She listened to everyone who wanted to talk to her, and observed every step of the production line. She seemed to really care about what everyone had to say. One day, she showed up in work clothes and joined in cleaning, slicing, and packaging. Initially, the workers and supervisors couldn't believe what they were seeing, but after a while they had accepted her as one of them.

Over the following weeks, the new owner continued to drop in and chat with people, and conditions began to change. Nearly all of these changes were the direct or indirect result of the suggestions offered by the staff, e.g.:

—The height of one of the cutting tables was lowered, and several of the shorter workers were moved to this table. [*Complaints of shoulder and back pains were dramatically reduced.*]

—Abrasive soaps were replaced by gentle but effective cleaning agents and lotions. [*The workers washed their hands and utensils more frequently.*]

—Workers were encouraged to begin cleaning up their tables 15 minutes before quitting time. [*The entire plant was cleaner.*]

—The supervisors were trained in leadership techniques, and their titles were changed to "team leaders." [*One team leader was promoted to manager, two workers were promoted to team leader, and job applications poured in.*]

—A better quality of chicken was used. [*A better quality of product was produced.*]

—Salaries were increased modestly. [*Sales increased significantly.*]

The team leaders began to really understand their role as teachers and facilitators and came up with a number of additional suggestions. Flex time was introduced, benefits were improved, and better equipment was purchased. Two years after purchasing the plant the owner sold it for three and a half times its original cost.

The Tactics of Leadership

> The horse never knows I'm there until he needs to.
> —Willie Shoemaker (jockey)

A good leader knows when to exhibit leadership, when to be a team player, and when to follow someone else's lead. Business and community leaders, teachers, parents, coaches, and jockeys all need to recognize the right time to pull the reins and when to leave them slack.

Leading

> To lead the people, walk behind them.
> —Lao-tzu

A leader's job is not to judge people but to determine who is in need of special help and to make sure that person receives it. A leader should focus on identifying the causes of a problem and then work to eliminate them. A leader nurtures cooperation and eliminates barriers to cooperation and to enjoyment of work.

The leader motivates by giving credit and by providing positive and (when necessary) negative reinforcement. The leader teaches by identifying and clarifying needs. The leader supplies energy with enthusiasm and by example. And when leadership is not needed, the leader lets loose the reins.

Following

A clever tail can wag the dog.

In theory, the current leader encourages others to assume leadership roles and moves into the background as they emerge. In practice, however, it can be difficult to give up what you've worked so hard to gain. Having enjoyed success and recognition as a leader, many people strive to keep the reins of power by dominating the upstarts who appear to threaten their status. At the same time, energetic and creative employees may not be satisfied to quietly follow established leaders.

CAREER BUSTER 5

BEING REACTIVE ALLOWS OTHERS TO CONTROL YOUR PATH

> Just about anything that can happen will happen, if you let it.

Reaction is response to something else. The more you react to what is initiated by others, the less you initiate yourself. The more reactive you become, the less control you exercise over the decisions and events that affect your life.

Reactive means lacking control and vulnerable to the hazard of invisible designs and agendas. Proactive people are those who employ their own restraints. In this manner they control the details that influence their lives while diminishing the control others may wield over them. The distinction between *proactive* and *reactive* is the difference between determining your own direction and meekly following the path set for you by outside interests.

The idea of control evokes images of domination, command, and authority—we think of generals and prison guards, of setting agendas and priorities, initiating actions, and running things our way. Actually, these are the popular but lesser aspects of control, whose major function is *to limit power*. Think of control as anti-power, a restraining influence upon the exercise of power over you.

As power is the *ability to do* (Chapter 15), control weakens that ability by immersing it in minutiae and making it more difficult to get things done. The main difference between power and control is *detail*: The power type is focused first upon the outcome and second (if at all) on the process; the control freak needs to be aware of every step and procedure along the way, and is less concerned about the outcome.

The tug-of-war between control and power has historic roots and very modern fruit. Machiavelli's method for governing events was through controlling the controllers. He believed that the unpredictable nature of events could be reduced, i.e., controlled to a degree, by limiting the control of others. Today, organizations do their best to shackle power through procedures, accountability, security, and hidden cameras. Responsibilities and privileges are carefully delimited, and important decisions are made by groups or committees. Written laws control the speed at which we are allowed to drive, the taxes we must pay, even some rather private details of our behavior; unwritten rules regulate the way we dress and speak and direct our eyes.

We are controlled from cradle to grave by those who wield the power of control, and we continuously seek to limit their power over us by subjecting them, in turn, to ever more control. It follows that, in order to proactively exercise control over our own lives and careers, we need to limit the control of others over us.

CAREER SAVERS
The Art of Control
The Tactics of Control

The Art of Control

> Control governs more by veto than by leadership.
> —James Hillman

Psychoanalyst James Hillman emphasizes the preventative nature of control. He describes control as the removal of obstacles: not being bothered, not being criticized, not being restricted. "Control means preventing interference," Hillman says, "so we feel frustrated by people in control."

Reactive types tend to accept controls unchallenged. They may gripe and moan, but they manage to live within them. The instinctive response of the proactive individual is to seek to break free of obstacles. Depending on the circumstances and people involved, it may be possible to circumvent or simply ignore certain restrictions. However, the safer and more lasting way to overcome controls is to weaken or eliminate them by controlling the people who impose them.

Self-Control

> The beauty of control is that you can apply the same
> principles and techniques you use on others to yourself.

Self-control is not allowing yourself to get sidetracked by temptation, inconvenience, discomfort, or doubt. It means refusing to accept at face value the advice, opinions, and constraints imposed by others. It means limiting your pursuit of useless (if enjoyable) activity in order to focus on important details (no matter how small). It means being willing to stand alone and, when necessary, to make the sacrifices that are the price of succeeding at anything worthwhile. Self-control can give you the confidence to believe in yourself, and that's the point from which you can begin to exercise control over the direction of your career.

> Controlling our thoughts is the key to gaining control over our lives.

You don't get to be a competent musician, computer programmer, architect, police officer, or surgeon without sacrifice. Even sports and fitness programs have their cost. Successful people are those who have the self-control to make the sacrifices and, when necessary, to overcome the blind pursuit of instant gratification, pleasure, and avoidance of the unpleasant in order to be successful.

> All sane people fear.

Control allows us to overcome the paralysis of fear—to confront, accommodate, and even use our fear to motivate us in a direction of our choosing.

> Back in the late 1970's, a close friend who used to work in the educational publishing business noticed an increasing number of computer terminals on people's desks. The more he encountered them, the more his ignorance of these electronic devices made him uncomfortable. One day, as he strolled past New York City's famous Museum of Natural History, he had a vision of himself, stuffed and mounted, in the dinosaur section. "That's where they'll put me five years from now," he muttered to himself, "if I don't learn about these computers."
>
> He spoke to a few employment agents and leveraged his business and communication skills to obtain a job in a computer software company. "I gave up the comfort of a familiar profession and a third of my salary to dive into the most foreign environment I had ever encountered. Everybody spoke in jargon and acronyms I'd never heard before, and I felt like a swimmer drowning in an ocean of alphabet soup with no sign of land; I was terribly uncomfortable and insecure. The only thing that kept me going, from giving up this mad experiment and rushing back to publishing, was fear of failure .. and the dinosaurs. Motivated by this fear I asked questions, took notes, and studied. I took people to lunch (they're a lot more tolerant when someone else is picking up the tab), developed friendships, and worked my butt off. I learned."

Today, our friend is a successful consultant with a good deal of control over his career. "I meet people every day who envy my income and independence. Some of them are a lot smarter than me .. but they're afraid to give up the security of their salaried positions." Their fear is in control.

In Control

> ..when a crisis occurs or is in the process of occurring, don't react. Just say you'd like to think about it.
> —Mark H. McCormack

Timing (Chapter 14) is one of the major considerations in acting and reacting wisely. If you respond too quickly to a situation, you risk being limited and carried away by someone else's initiative. The right time to act is usually when you've had a chance to formulate your response in your own terms. On the other hand, waiting too long to provide your input can leave you out of the decision loop. For if you sit back and wait for things to happen, eventually they will—they'll happen to you, around you, and in spite of you. You have a better chance of influencing the events and decisions that affect your life and career by playing a more active role in them. How can you exercise more control over these circumstances?

The art of being in control begins with establishing priorities. Since you cannot possibly control everything, you must determine what is worth controlling, and the degree to which control is feasible.

> The amount of available information doubles every five years.

As in most areas, you have to decide what is really important to you and what is not. Are you mostly concerned with profits, costs, production, quality, or something else? Are you too busy and preoccupied with popular trends and values to figure out what is working against you and holding you back?

Out of Control.   There are two ways to be out of control: by allowing others to dictate your priorities and direction, and by losing sight of what really matters to you. People who get caught up in needing to control everything are as much out of control as those who allow themselves to be led about like sheep. Being out of control is helplessness, even if you are the chairman of the board.

The Tactics of Control

> The puppeteer controls the performance by pulling the
> right strings. By responding to the strings, the puppet
> controls the movements of the puppeteer.

Reward and Punishment

> The Lord giveth, and the Lord taketh away.

The principle of the carrot applies to most living things. We are
conditioned to reward and punishment controls from childhood:
Do this, and that will follow; don't do this, or that will happen.
This technique is used to motivate, direct, and limit our behavior
at home, at school, at play, and later on at work. However, each
of us responds differently to different kinds of motivation and
restriction.

An example is provided by the reasons for not running a traffic light: It's against the law; if you get caught you may receive a
traffic ticket; it's dangerous—you might have an accident. The
point is that we need to identify the tactics and conditions that we
and those around us respond to most strongly in order to exercise
some control over ourselves and the environments in which we
function.

Imposing Controls

> The way to deal with a strong ego—yours or someone
> else's—is to examine it, understand it, and then control it.

Other than reward and punishment, the most popular techniques for
imposing controls are established rules and the imposition of trust.
The reason we do not include *fear* in this category is that it is largely unreliable and impractical. Threats and other fear-inducing tactics
may serve to control some people, but they are more likely to antag-
onize people.

Trust is often an effective tactic in gaining the loyalty of colleagues and subordinates. By convincing others that we trust and
rely on them, we seek to bond them to us as allies and supporters.
Clichés are used to elicit trust from those over whom we wish to
gain control: "I'm sure that I can count on you." "Can I rely on
you to help?" "You do right by me, and I'll take care of you."
"Trust me ..."

Seats of Control.   Determining priorities, as by setting the agenda, is another effective tactic of control. Like leading, this prerogative can be exercised from different vantage points.

Information

> Holding a certain amount of critical information in reserve about how you plan to execute a project or solve a problem is one of the cornerstones of power.
> —Michael Korda

Korda's formula is to reveal just enough to sell your idea without revealing the key elements that will make it work. This ensures that you maintain ownership of the plan, and that you receive full credit for implementing it. If you are responsible for amassing and organizing important data, take advantage of a golden opportunity to make it work for you. For example, you might produce a system that makes valuable information quickly available, but in a manner that is fully understood by no one else. In this way, those who come to depend upon the data will also have to depend on you.

Minutiae.   As we mentioned earlier, power addicts tend to focus on results rather than details, whereas control freaks want to be aware of everything that's going on. They insist on being kept up-to-date on the smallest of details, receiving copies of every document they can lay their hands on, and being included in the approval chain for all decisions, invoices, and such. Intentionally or inadvertently, their need to monitor events serves to diminish the power of those around them.

Maintaining Controls

> I will not participate in this deal unless I control it, pure and simple. No ifs, no ands and no buts.
> —Reginald F. Lewis [*Why Should White Guys Have All the Fun? Reginald F. Lewis & Blair S. Walker (Wiley), New York: 1995*]

The more there is at stake, the stronger the challenges to gain and maintain control.

During Reginald Lewis' successful billion-dollar acquisition of TLC Beatrice, he had to battle continually with the people from Drexel,

Burnham, Lambert (particularly Peter Ackerman), as well as with some of the banks, to remain in charge. It was important enough to Lewis that he be acknowledged as the head man that, at one point during the lengthy negotiations, he considered cutting Drexel (which was putting up about half the money) out of the deal completely. He used his eloquence, his force of personality, and when necessary, brinkmanship by threatening to pull out of the deal himself, in order to maintain personal control.

Once the deal was done, Lewis directed his energies toward managing the press to focus upon him, and not on the other players. After assuming control over the widespread entities owned by Beatrice, he visited them frequently, at times conducting business meetings in several countries on the same day. He worked hard and energetically to understand the details of his international empire, amassing a personal fortune of several hundred million dollars.

Lewis' urge to control extended to his home life: When he played tennis, the racquets and balls had to be in a certain place and position, the courtside umbrella just so. When he presided in his dining room, a hidden button under the table enabled him to send instructions to the butler so that the wine glasses were always filled and the dishes cleared exactly when he wished. When Lewis succumbed to brain cancer in January, 1993, he was buried with a box of his favorite cigars, a bottle of vintage champagne, and a tennis racquet .. just in case.

CAREER BUSTER 6

WITHOUT THE NECESSARY SKILLS
YOU'RE OUT OF LUCK

Men habitually use only a small part of the powers they
actually possess.
—William James

This chapter is about the personal qualities and skills that can help or damage your career. Although these two categories are arguably different, the qualities and skills discussed here fall under the common banner of career-related abilities.

Personal qualities, like confidence and honesty, are considered by many as a gift from parents, ancestors, or a higher power. However, many of these qualities can be acquired and improved in the same manner as skills. Our objective is to identify the abilities you need, help you to assess your strengths and weaknesses, and convince you that you can—and really should—improve your command of them. And so, talent aside, we shall treat all of these abilities as career-related skills that can be acquired and improved to some degree through concentrated effort in as little as a year. Since different careers make separate demands, we shall focus on the generic (universal) skills on which success in most occupations is based. We're not suggesting that you need all these skills in order to succeed, but that a lack of any one could turn into a career buster.

People often place the highest value on the attributes that helped them get ahead and those they personally wish they had more of. We have categorized these attributes into three interrelated groups: *personal qualities, interpersonal skills,* and specific *job-related skills.* These are the abilities that employers tend to value, and most of them can help you to empower your career. Most of them are so important that entire chapters have been devoted to them in this book.

CAREER SAVERS

Personal Qualities
Interpersonal Skills
Job-Related Skills
Self-Evaluation

Personal Qualities

> I am one of the few honest people that I have ever
> known.
> —Francis Scott Fitzgerald (*The Great Gatsby*)

Our list of personal qualities focuses on self-confidence, intregity, motivation, vision, judgment, flexibility, problem-solving ability, entrepreneurship, a positive attitude, and ability to learn.

Self-Confidence

> Little minds are tamed and subdued by misfortunes, but
> great minds rise above them.
> —Washington Irving

Self-confidence (Chapter 1) is as important to feel as to exude. Without confidence in your ability to perform and grow, you become the most formidable obstacle to your own success. And without a public image of confidence, others will be reluctant to entrust you with responsibilities that may reflect upon them.

Integrity

> Assume a virtue, if you have it not.
> —William Shakespeare (*Hamlet*)

Integrity (Chapter 7) is an essential element in winning the trust and confidence of employers, colleagues, and clients. No matter how skilled and experienced you may be in your profession, people who have reason to question your credibility, reliability, and honesty will discourage people from associating with you.

Motivation

> Poverty makes for more eager learners than does
> privilege ...
> —journalist Farah Baria (New Delhi)

Progress takes effort. Whether you need to brush up on some skills or plan a major realignment, it's up to you to make the effort. The reward awaiting an informed and focused effort is the satisfaction of personal and career growth, and the knowledge that you've got what it takes to make and to sustain that effort.

Seven-year-old Raju (he doesn't know his last name) is a shoe shine boy in Bombay, India. Raju is ambitious, taking advantage of a special volunteer school conducted by a devoted couple on the platform of Bombay's Andheri train station. Like many of his fellow students—rag pickers, flower sellers, and beggars ranging in age from 3 to 12—he learns, works, and sleeps right on the station platform. During working hours, Raju approaches customers with his cloth, shoe polish, and newly acquired professional courtesy: "Excuse me, sir, do you want boot polish?" His personal brand of polish, contrasted to that of his competitors, earns him higher tips and a measure of respect. A classmate, nine-year-old Kavita, sells flowers at a nearby traffic light. "When I learn to read and write," she smiles hopefully, "I can get a job in an office." And Dangubai, eleven, announced recently, "I want to stop begging and begin a new life." Her determined voice was barely audible above the roar of an incoming train.

Vision

> For I dipped into the future, far as human eye could see,
> Saw the vision of the world, and all the wonder that
> would be.
> —Alfred, Lord Tennyson

Vision is the product of self-confidence, discipline, energy, motivation, and inspiration. It is considered an intangible quality in that it's difficult to define why some people have it and others don't. The imagination to see things as they might be and to bring them about are highly prized abilities. Yet even such uncommon abilities can be enhanced through the self-confidence of believing in your vision, the credibility that encourages others to listen to your ideas, priorities that give your imagination some direction, a sensitivity to your work environment, networking skills (Chapter 16) that enable you to become aware of the goals and problems of your company, and the motivation that encourages you to try.

Judgment

> Common sense is not so common.
> —Voltaire

Judgement skills—also known as common sense—are largely based on intelligence (which most of us have), experience (which most of us can gain), and planning (Chapters 9 and 21), which most of us are capable of if we're willing to invest the time and effort. It helps to focus upon the issue at hand, solicit other opinions and perspectives, and research any similar situations that may have occurred in the past.

Flexibility

> Progress is impossible without change, and those who cannot change their minds cannot change anything.
> —George Bernard Shaw

A closed mind is an inflexible mind. We are frustrated when we encounter stubbornness in others, and often unaware when others find it in us. Inflexibility is a barrier to a satisfying and successful career. Adaptability is a prime survival mechanism and a necessary element of vision, flexibility, and problem solving.

One of the reasons for the legendary Bob Hope's success over an amazing 50-year career as an entertainer was his willingness to adjust to change. Starting out in vaudeville, Hope made the adjustment to Broadway, film, radio, and television as each came into vogue. The names of entertainers who could or would not make similar adjustments have been relegated to games of trivia and unread memoirs.

In the early stages of a career, the enormous challenges that face us are mitigated by an abundance of youthful energy and optimism. As habits become entrenched over time, there is a tendency to hold on to what got us where we are and a reluctance to interrupt the patterns that we have grown familiar with ..and that inhibit change. However, what worked in the past may not serve the future. As Charles Handy wrote in *The Age of Unreason,* "Change is not what it used to be. The status quo will no longer be the best way forward. The best way will be less comfortable and less easy, but no doubt, more interesting—a word we often use to signal an uncertain mix of danger and opportunity." In other words, nothing lasts forever, except, perhaps, change.

Problem-Solving Ability

> Everything has two handles—by one of which it ought to be carried and by the other not.
> —Epictetus

Recent U.S. Labor Department studies have identified a growing demand for problem-solving abilities in the workforce. Problem solving depends upon reliable information, relevant experience, vision, flexibility, and motivation: If you really want or need to solve a problem, you are more likely to focus all of your abilities on doing so. The way you learn from past mistakes (Chapter 10) is the basis of your ability to solve the problems of the future.

Entrepreneurship

> Entrepreneurs are those who perceive what others fail to see.

Control Data, General Motors, IBM, Polaroid, Texas Instruments, and Xerox are only a few of the many major corporations created by a single individual who had an idea and carried it through. Clarence Birdseye (working as a fur trader in Labrador) noticed that when fish, caribou, geese, and cabbage were quickly frozen in the sub-zero temperatures outside his cabin during the Canadian winters, they still tasted pretty good after they were thawed. This led to the creation of a multibillion dollar industry.

Entrepreneurship is taking problem solving to the next level, that of recognizing needs and seeking creative and practical solutions. Entrepreneurs are open to new ideas and ways of looking at things; they are highly motivated, and generally prefer working for themselves.

Positive Attitude

> If one advances confidently in the direction of his dreams, and endeavors to live the life which he has imagined, he will meet with a success unexpected in common hours.
> —Henry David Thoreau

Positive energy (Chapter 1) can spark the confidence and persistence to achieve your greatest ambitions. The level of your expectation of success tends to be self-filling: small, medium, or large. A positive mental attitude (PMA) is essential to being a good communicator (Chapter 2), leader (Chapter 4), learner, and problem solver.

Malcolm Boyd (*Modern Maturity,* June-July 1993) suggests that a positive approach to dealing with problems can lead to constructive solutions, and many reliable medical authorities have documented the power of positive thinking to overcome serious health problems. Clearly, a positive, can-do attitude is helpful, if not necessary, to achieve the difficult and seemingly impossible tasks that we manage to accomplish throughout our careers and lives.

Ability to Learn

> Give me a spark o' Nature's fire, That's the learning I
> desire.
> —Robert Burns

The ability and willingness to learn and apply new skills, innovative methodologies, and imaginative solutions is absolutely essential in a world of blossoming and rapidly changing technologies. "Having a willingness to learn and good interpersonal skills are more important than technical skills," says Professor Charles Fay of the Rutgers University School of Management and Labor Relations. Learning to learn is also at the top of the American Society for Training and Development's list of skills identified as crucial by employers.

Interpersonal Skills

> While all people want and need to be liked by some of
> the people some of the time, it is only the modern other-
> directed types who make this their chief source of
> direction and chief area of sensitivity.
> —David

There is a natural tendency for people to weight skills according to their industry: Communication skills are obviously vital to journalists, analytical thinking is essential to engineers, and persuasive abilities are required by politicians. What many people overlook is the fact that these and many other skills are prerequisites to success in almost any field.

The U.S. Labor Department projects that highly specialized functions (like computer programming) are beginning to give way to jobs that require interpersonal skills and a good deal of flexibility. Everywhere we go—in both the public and private sectors—we hear repeatedly that good interpersonal skills are increasingly in demand. Our list of interpersonal skills is made up of communication, persuasiveness, leadership, and charisma or charm. The most important of these to your career are the ones you have; the most important ones to acquire are those you lack and that are limiting your progress.

Many people believe that as they continue to work hard, their lack of interpersonal skills won't hurt them. But when budget crunches and major shake-ups occur, the contributions of a quiet worker may be overlooked by executives concentrating on financial and political considerations. And they (the quiet ones) are often passed over for promotions, new equipment, and better facilities. Even the most talented professionals eventually discover how improved interpersonal skills could have enhanced their careers.

Communication

> I'll pay more for a man's ability to express himself than for any other quality he might possess.
> —Charles Schwab

Communication skills (Chapter 2) are not only the means to convey your ideas, plans, results, and ambitions; they are also the basis of a good number of careers. Salespeople, executives, lawyers, and teachers are just a few of the professionals that rely on excellent communications. Add to the list anyone who needs to conduct productive meetings, make presentations, provide leadership, negotiate, solicit backing and cooperation, and—let's not forget—interview and network.

Persuasiveness. The ability to influence relies on good communication skills, preparation, and an understanding of whomever you are trying to persuade. It is used to obtain and keep a job, to earn promotions and raises, to market ideas, products, and services, to elicit cooperation and support, to motivate others, and generally to get your way. Among equally qualified candidates, generally the one who gets the salary increase, project, grant, larger office, better equipment, recognition, and other perks is the one who does the best job of convincing the decision makers to decide in her favor.

Leadership. Leadership (Chapter 4) is the process of motivating and coordinating people toward a common purpose. Effective leaders have an abundance of persistence, individualism, and the ability to think critically. They also need to be effective communicators, motivators, and teachers, to establish reasonable priorities, and possess strong persuasive skills.

Charisma

> Charm is the ability to very quickly make a great impression on practically anyone.
> —Michael W. Mercer

Charisma is the ability to make people feel comfortable around you and want to associate with you. By itself it is an empty promise; but it can make the difference between which of several equal candidates gets the job and the best opportunities. Few employers ask for or list charisma or charm among their job requirements, but it is not to be overlooked as a career asset. For the most part, charisma is the product of self-confidence, public image, communication skills, and a pleasant nature. If you find that you seem to rub certain people the wrong way, you may need to find out more about the image you have of yourself and the one that you're projecting.

Job-Related Skills

> Half your skills become obsolete every four to six years.

Our list of job-related skills falls into two groups: the technical skills, which tend to rely less on communication and other interpersonal skills and more on mental and manual ability; and the functional skills needed by most companies. We added job-getting skills to emphasize the importance of both interviewing and networking.

Technical Skills

> Where have all the plumbers gone?

Most technical skills are industry-defined. Photography, driving, mechanical repairs, sketching, carpentry, cooking, and computer programming are among the many skills that can enable you to find employment nearly anywhere. In fact, a large percentage of recent immigrants to North America find employment in these areas. The disadvantage of relying on only one or two such skills is that it leaves most of the decisions that affect your job and career at the mercy of someone else's agenda.

Functional Skills

> ..the permanent disuse of any organ imperceptibly diminishes its functional capacity, until it finally disappears.
> —Jean Baptiste Lamarck

The functional skills, like managing, planning, assessing, prioritizing, negotiating, selling (marketing), presenting, negotiating, and computer literacy span a wider variety of fields and jobs. These too can be learned and improved on by most people who recognize the need and are willing to make the effort to do so. The most universal of these types of skills in today's marketplace are management and computer literacy, for just about every company has need of both.

Management is discussed and contrasted to leadership in Chapter 4. Every company, whether it produces or markets products or services, needs good management. Given a knowledge of the industry or business, management skills are often readily transferable to different departments and companies.

> The factory of the future will have only two employees, a man and a dog. The man will be there to feed the dog. The dog will be there to keep the man from touching the equipment.
> —Warren G. Bennis

Computer skills span nearly every profession. Secretaries and clerks as well as technical people and executives use them to input data and produce correspondence and reports, access massive databases, store and transfer information, perform calculations, project budgets, communicate with other on- and off-site data centers, and numerous other purposes. The more you understand about the functional capabilities of computers, the better equipped you'll be to address the needs of your department and company in almost any business. Aside from manual labor, it is hard to imagine very many career paths in which at least the most basic computer skills are not and will not be needed in the very near future.

Job-Getting Skills

> Everything that is hard to attain is easily assailed ...
> —Ptolemy

To use your skills on the job, you must first get the job. This means finding the job you want and then convincing someone to hire you.

Networking (Chapter 16) is the vehicle by which the overwhelming majority of jobs are found. It's tough to navigate the job market on your own. If you don't know how (or are unwilling to make the effort) to network, you risk missing out on people and spheres of influence that may help you to find a job, support your business, and enhance your career.

> Most people who fail to get the job they really want fail
> not because they are not qualified but because they failed
> in the interview. And most failure occurs because they
> aren't prepared.
> —David W. Crawley, Jr.

Interviewing skills (Chapter 20) are needed not only to get a job, but
also to help earn promotions, raises, and recognition. A successful
interview requires solid preparation (Chapter 21) and good communication (especially listening) skills (Chapter 2).

Self-Evaluation

Your assessment of your strengths and defects may be accurate or
self-indulgent. Is your career progressing as well and quickly as you
might reasonably expect? Is it moving in the direction of your choosing? Take a quick reality check and look at your work environment.
How do you, in your own view, fit in? Do you get along well with
your colleagues and boss? Are you chosen for important assignments? Are your accomplishments generally appreciated? Is your
hard work rewarded with raises and promotions? Or are you on a
treadmill, running just to stay in place?

Focus in on your colleagues and on acquaintances in other lines
of work—especially the ones who appear to be pulling ahead. Are
they better organizers, communicators, motivators? Do they appear
more confident and self-assured? What have they got more of than
you? Do they exhibit certain qualities that give them an advantage?
Make a list of these assets. Discuss them with a supervisor, a job
counselor, even some of those successful individuals, and prioritize
your list. Can you acquire some the abilities you lack and improve
on the ones you already own to some degree? Of course you can ...
maybe not 100% of them, but most. Once you recognize the need,
all it takes is planning and an effort on your part.

Using What You Have

> The warrior is the one who uses the pen and the sword
> with equal skill.
> —Miyomoto Musashi (16th Century Japanese swordmaster)

It is natural to emphasize your strengths and leverage your existing
skills. Of course you want to put your best self forward in pursuing
career objectives. Job placement and human resource professionals

universally guide their clients and candidates toward careers in keeping with their current abilities. We are tested from cradle to grave in order to assess our abilities and interests. As a result, most of us discover early in life—often before we're out of school or college—the *right* and *wrong* areas for us to follow. In many cases, we buy in to these assessments of our present and future capabilities long before we have even begun to approach our true potential, and simply go with the flow. We continue doing what we've always been good at, and avoid the areas of our weakness or ignorance.

This formula works better for some than others. If you're pleased with your career, congratulations! But if you are less than satisfied, you might benefit from a reassessment of your objectives and your skills. Highly competent workers often get held back because management considers them quite useful where they are. These workers may even be better paid than supervisors and managers at the lower end of the next higher level. But if they want to get promoted, perhaps to branch out into management, good communication skills could help them to express their wishes to their bosses and enhance their qualifications for the move.

Acquiring What You Need

> I have learned silence from the talkative, toleration from
> the intolerant, and kindness from the unkind.
> —Kahlil Gibran

The most direct way to determine which skills you may be lacking, or those you need to sharpen, is by observing people who are where you want to be. What skills does your objective require? How do your own abilities compare with those of people who are in similar positions? Draw encouragement from the skills you share, identify the ones you lack, and make up your mind to acquire and improve on the ones you need.

▼▼▼

CAREER BUSTER 7

INDISCRETIONS NULLIFY YOUR BEST INTENTIONS

People do the worst of things for the best of reasons.

When business leaders are asked to name the qualities they value most in people, integrity is high on the majority of lists. The indiscretions against which they warn focus on honesty, the way we treat others, and the way we represent ourselves.

By "indiscretion" we mean any rash, inappropriate, or other unwise act that may give you reason for regret. This includes misrepresenting the truth, prejudice, cheating, harassment, arrogance, bad-mouthing, aggravating, alienating, exaggerated dress and grooming, pretentious utterances (in poor taste, inaccurate, or both), and other such exercises of poor judgment. Anyone can make a mistake; the difference is that an indiscretion is more likely to be the natural product of an attitude or blind spot than a random occurrence from which we may choose to learn and grow.

CAREER SAVERS

The Art of Common Sense
The Tactics of Discretion

The Art of Common Sense

I've noticed that nothing I never said has hurt me.
—Calvin Coolidge

Treating others as you would prefer to be treated is a practical philosophy. Actions tend to generate similar reactions, and people are often treated in accordance with their own behavior. When we deal with other humans, we make judgments based on what we see and hear. These observations lead us to like, dislike, trust, or distrust certain people, just as we are evaluated by them.

51

Ethical Behavior

> If you know it's wrong, don't do it. If you believe that
> others think it's wrong, reflect upon it carefully. If it is
> likely to hurt someone, seek an alternative.

Doing the right thing requires an open mind; not doing the wrong thing merely requires caution, intelligence, and information. A simple rule of thumb for deciding whether or not to commit an action is to consider it from opposing points of view. First, how do you feel about it? Does it seem wrong? Look at it from the other side: How do you anticipate someone else might react to your doing it? If you're not sure, you can always ask a friend or trusted colleague. Then ask yourself how you would feel if someone else did it. Finally, try to project the likely outcome if you decide not to do it.

Unethical Behavior

> The essence of lying is in deception, not in words.
> —John Ruskin

Since the majority of us read little more than local and national newspapers and journals, let us point out that unethical behaviors are occurring everywhere in recognizably familiar patterns. As telecommunications and computer systems and the entertainment media "normalize" and link the nations of our world with common goals and the means for attaining them, the pressures and problems of pursuing a successful career are similar in Baltimore, Brussels, and Brisbane. Overpopulation and increasing competition for a limited number of jobs and shrinking resources are lamented daily in a thousand dialects. In every occupation, conflicts and temptations challenge common sense and ethics. Wherever you go, the patterns are analogous. The same qualities that are admired in Taipei are valued in Topeka, and the very same indiscretions can get you into trouble. The following tale has its counterpart in every city and every profession.

> There's a story going around about a cigar smoker who bought a very
> expensive box of cigars and had them insured against fire. After smoking
> them all, he filed a claim with the insurance company, for the cigars had
> indeed been consumed by fire. To teach the unscrupulous fellow a lesson
> the insurers decided to honor the claim. But when he tried to collect
> the money, he was arrested for arson.

Integrity

> If everyone were clothed with integrity, if every heart
> were just, frank, kindly, the other virtues would be
> essentially useless, since their chief purpose is to make us
> bear with patience the injustice of our fellows.
> —Molière

People are less patient these days and far less tolerant of being mistreated. With dozens of qualified candidates ready to compete for a single opening, personal comportment and demeanor have grown in importance as job qualifications in many companies. Personality and credibility are often effective tiebreakers when other qualities appear more or less equal.

The Tactics of Discretion

> My first qualification for mayor of New York is my,
> monumental ingratitude to each and every one of you.
> —(former New York City mayor) Fiorello LaGuardia

It is difficult to talk about appropriate behavior and practices without contrasting them with their unseemly counterparts. And so, despite our preference for positive models, this chapter includes a number of descriptions and examples of the injudicious and ill-advised actions that have injured and destroyed so many careers.

Anatomy of an Indiscretion

> ..where ignorance is bliss, 'tis folly to be wise.
> —William Whitehead

Many people are unaware of the effects of their indiscretions on other people and themselves; otherwise they might behave more reasonably. Sometimes it's hard to recognize in ourselves the very same behavior we find objectionable in others.

> ..one should hate nobody whom one cannot destroy.
> —Goethe

Frustration is a predictable byproduct of intense competition. High levels of frustration are easily fanned into anger toward an individual or an organization. Disagreements and hurt feelings are commonplace—disgruntled workers have been known to shoot or bomb their former employers. People who do not get what they want or believe they deserve may feel that they are being treated unfairly. The resentment that results is focused on a target, or will seek one. Jealousy and righteous indignation have likely spawned more antisocial acts than any other cause.

Indifference is an advanced state of ignorance and indignation. It is difficult to remain indifferent when you recognize the likelihood of negative consequences; and it is unusual for people to consciously risk self-destruction unless motivated by an overwhelming sense of indignation.

These are the indiscretions that we and a lot of other people believe to be the most likely career busters.

Honesty remains a valued attribute. Recognize that if you are accused or strongly suspected of unlawful acts, your career may be a dead or wounded duck. Inflating expense accounts, accepting unauthorized payments, filching, pilfering, and all the other euphemisms for taking things that don't belong to you are potential grounds for dismissal and prosecution. Rationalizing illegal behavior is a euphoric delusion. If your moral compunctions do not protect you from such folly, an awareness of the consequences should suffice.

To users of illicit drugs and overusers of alcohol, we offer a single thought: Take a good, long look at the people who get caught up in these habits, and ask yourself, "Do I want to be like that?"

There is a tendency for abusive people to attempt to justify their insults or laugh them off as harmless humor. At best, harassment is an illegal, tasteless, and self-destructive practice; at worst it is the sign of a disturbed personality. The encouragement or acceptance of this behavior in others labels you as sharing its underlying attitudes.

Sexual harassment was the theme of author Michael Crichton's successful novel, *Disclosure.* A popular movie based on the book dramatized the conflicts encountered by a male employee confronted with the sexual advances of his avaricious female boss, and the resulting threat to both of their careers. Only in recent years have we seen a widespread recognition and acknowledgment of this degrading practice and a concentrated effort to combat it.

If the newspapers and TV programs accurately reflect our world, racial attitudes appear to be frozen in time. Although the workplace cannot entirely undo the prejudices people bring with them, it can offer a more equal playing field and an environment in which open minds can meet. Those who persist in religious, racial, ethnic, sexual, and other forms of harassment will find it increasingly difficult to thrive in all but the most isolated places, and who will mourn their passing?

It is a virtue to be deserving of your faults.
—Georg Christoph Lichtenberg

It is normal to develop friendships with colleagues and associates. There is, however, a "line of propriety" that is safer uncrossed. This includes dating (or contributing even to the impression of a sexual liaison) and financial transactions (borrowing, investing, or selling costly items). The reasons are fairly obvious: Both contain the potential for special treatment that may be unfair to coworkers, as well as the seeds of an unpleasant aftermath.

There's a big difference between knowing what you're talking about and representing a mere theory as a fact. People aren't as easily fooled as you may think, and they can usually tell when you're not being entirely truthful. Exaggeration, fabrication, and other forms of deception are little more than lying; and once you earn a reputation as a liar, you might as well seek greener pastures elsewhere.

Unplanned outbursts of emotion can be devastating to a career. Nobody wants to deal with people who are known to blow their cool, and overly emotive types are rarely entrusted with important managerial or decision-making positions.

Vindictiveness is an intense temptation that rarely works in your favor. In team sports, the player who retaliates for an unseen shove or blow is usually the one called for the penalty. In an office environment, the colleague who does you dirty is probably more gifted at giving hurt than you. Nor is your career well served by devoting much time and effort into developing this particular talent.

Progress is often described as three steps forward and two steps backward. If you poison the path and the resources that got you where you are today, the option of a temporary, tactical retreat may not be available to you. Remember too that many of the people you meet along the way are moving in the same general direction as you, and one never knows when paths may cross.

Arrogance and related manifestations of superiority are considered antisocial forms of behavior in most environments. Looking down at people rarely induces them to look up at you. According to Richard Seely, the accounting manager of a Rapid City fast-food enterprise, "Arrogance is the greatest career buster. How can you talk to or deal with someone who thinks he knows everything? Why would you even want to try?"

A chicken in every pot and two cars in every garage.
—Herbert Hoover

Failing to keep your word destroys credibility and, eventually, the likelihood of others keeping their promises to you. If people cannot count on you, your value as a member of their team is compromised.

If you are privy to privileged information, keep it to yourself. Divulging confidential information is betrayal of a trust, whether of an individual or a corporation. Those to whom the informer tells his secrets are the first to know him for a traitor.

Absenteeism and tardiness are equated with a lack of reliability and dedication to one's job and company. Exceptional circumstances, such as family obligations or physical conditions, may create the need for special arrangements. Otherwise, unexpected absences and chronic lateness are universally unacceptable. Other forms of unreliability include failing to keep your word, not being there for others when they need you, and doing less than what is expected of you.

> I do not resent criticism, even when, for the sake of emphasis, it parts for the time with reality.
> —Winston Churchill

The personnel manager of an Omaha bank underlines one's ability to accept criticism as a vital career building block. "Nobody enjoys being criticized, but if you can't take criticism, there's a lot about yourself you'll never learn."

> People ask you for criticism, but they only want praise.
> —William Somerset Maugham

As important as it is to consider and learn from valid criticism, critiquing someone else is a delicate issue. A person who is insulted by, angered by, or fearful of your criticism is more likely to react to her emotion than to consider the constructive elements. She may resent you instead of appreciating your effort.

Before you offer criticism, determine if your target is open to hearing it. Did he ask for it? Do you have a relationship of trust and respect with this person? How has she reacted to criticism in the past? Have you ever accepted criticism from him? Make sure no one else can overhear the conversation, and be prepared to make your point as clearly and briefly as possible. Focus on a single point; don't overexplain, repeat yourself, or argue; try to be supportive of the other person by referring to a positive accomplishment or trait.

Criticizing people behind their backs is ill-advised. Not only are they likely to find out about it, but what they hear may be worse than what you really said.

If you tend to dominate conversations, you will find yourself ignored or interrupted every now and then. Likewise, when another person tries to dominate, you have every right to cut in on them politely and firmly: "You know, the point you've been making reminded me of something you might like to hear."

"The worst thing about kissing butt," Seattle aeronautical engineer Jane M. tells us, "is that after a while you begin to look like one. I mean, everybody knows you're doing it, and you just look ridiculous." So if you absolutely must play up to the boss, at least do it discreetly.

It is imprudent to reveal details about yourself or others that could cause you grief. If you are willing to share a secret with a colleague, what is there to stop them from "confiding" in a few of their own cronies? Are you willing to rely on someone else's sense of propriety? Of course, there are individuals who will keep your trust, but once you have divulged a confidence, you are no longer its exclusive owner.

> I think Comrade Gorbachev is a little nervous about me.
> Yes, unfortunately I think he has the idea I want his job.
> —Boris Yeltsin (in 1989)

End-running your boss is more likely to get you in trouble than not. A former manager of one of the world's largest consulting services firms explains how a pair of new staff members killed whatever chance they might have had at a career within that organization.

> Loyalty is the key to both getting a job and keeping it.
> —John Wareham

A loyal employee creates no unpleasant surprises and avoids embarassing the boss. Today, so many people change jobs and companies so often, loyalty may be lost in the mix. While it is difficult to feign devotion to a company or boss, it is useful to speak and behave like a loyal employee. After all, doesn't the organization that pays your salary and other benefits deserve *some* form of consideration from you?

Company rules and regulations were enacted for a reason. The original purpose may no longer be valid, or you may find it objectionable, but that is not the point. The bottom line is that violating corporate policy may be cause for dismissal, even if the act is not illegal. For example, many corporations take their dress and grooming codes quite seriously, and to show up in certain offices wearing a warmup suit or nose ring is asking for the door. Flouting official or tacit regulations is generally taken as rebellion, and if management lets one person get away with it, the policy is defunct. The people who are entrusted with creating and approving rules may decide to change them, but probably not for the sole purpose of accommodating you. Here are a few amusing errors for which their speakers have been rather embarassed.

> Trees cause more pollution than automobiles.
> —Ronald Reagan (in 1981)

President Reagan also confused his hosts (in Brazil) as *the people of Bolivia*; British Labour Party leader Denis Healy as *Mr. Ambassador* (the Ambassador, whom Reagan had just met, was standing nearby); Liberian leader Samuel Doe (in the White House) as *Chairman Moe*; and Princess Diana as *Princess David*.

> I think we're on the road to coming up with answers that I don't think any of us in total feel we have the answers to.
> —Kim Anderson (mayor of Naples, Florida, in 1991)

> Capital punishment is our society's recognition of the sanctity of life.
> —(Utah senator) Orrin Hatch (in 1988)

> [Republicans] understand the importance of bondage between parent and child.
> —Dan Quayle (He probably meant *bonding*.)

Of course, anyone can make a mistake, although a repeated pattern of inaccurate and thoughtless comments can make you a liability to your employer.

Your table manners during a business lunch, munching on a sandwich in the company cafeteria, or sipping coffee at someone's desk won't win you many jobs, but they very well may lose you a promotion. When violations of etiquette occur during an interview they can leave lasting stains. One professional recruiter (*National Business Employment Weekly*, May 7-13, 1995) described an interviewee pulling with his fingers at the cheese in his french onion soup; another spoke of a candidate for a medical director's position ordering a second main course (lobster after steak) while dining with the client.

▼▼▼

Your choice of language and physical appearance advertise your attitudes and values. A neat and tidy image is universally preferred by factory managers, public service employers, and corporate executives alike. Your line of work may not require you to dress and groom yourself with fastidious impeccability, but soiled, crumpled, or poorly-fitted clothing and unseemly personal hygiene are detriments to most careers.

CAREER BUSTER 8

STRESS AND POOR HEALTH CAN RENDER YOU UNABLE TO COMPETE

..health is the greatest of human blessings ...
—Hippocrates

Stress is the most notorious cause of career-induced illness. All the books, lectures, classes, and clinics devoted to reducing stress boil down to a single theme: The conditions that can cause stress are all around you and cannot be eliminated, so it's up to you to deal with them if you wish to have a healthy career and life.

Stress isn't the only reason for poor health—genetics, neglect, and ignorance also play major roles. Despite a wealth of information on healthy foods and activities, there is ample evidence that many people in all professions continue to overlook or ignore the importance of fitness in pursuing a successful career.

CAREER SAVERS
The Art of Handling Stress
The Tactics of Good Health

The Art of Handling Stress

You're only here for a short visit. Don't hurry. Don't worry. And be sure to smell the flowers along the way.
—Walter C. Hagen

Understanding Stress. Stress is an important part of the mental alarm system. Just as pain warns us of physical damage, stress alerts us to the possibility of having to deal with an imminent threat. Short-term stress can produce a burst of energy enabling us to overcome an immediate or perceived danger. Over the long term, however, it may leave us in a cardiology care unit.

According to Dr. Robert S. Eliot, Director of the Institute of Stress Medicine, Jackson Hole (Wyoming), stress encourages the release of two strong chemicals by the brain: cortisol and adrenalin.

The continuous or frequent presence of these two chemicals in the bloodstream can cause several health-threatening complications by raising blood pressure and releasing blood-clotting agents. These can damage the cardiovascular, immune, and respiratory systems, as well as the gastrointestinal tract, leading to heart disease, strokes, ulcers, and related complications.

Stress runs high in certain professions. Houston trauma surgeon James "Red" Duke, who was highly touted for the office of Attorney General a few years back, has trained his body to cope when his mind is occupied with helping other bodies. His resting pulse rate of 69 drops as low as 54 during particularly stressful sessions, an excellent form of self-defense. "Hell," Duke exclaims, "I have more fun working and doing the stuff I do than most people do paying a lot of money to go on a vacation."

The most common signs of ongoing stress are insomnia, fatigue, irritability, anger, frustration, pessimism, and poor health habits (like smoking, excessive drinking, drug abuse, overeating, malnutrition, and so on). In some cases it results in severe depression, suicide, or brutality toward others. Long-term stress is one of the most powerful ways that an unhealthy mind can poison an otherwise healthy body.

Stress is the mind's response to problems it feels unable to resolve. This conflict is often motivated by crises and complications at work or home, or even the anticipation of a problem. The illness of a family member, marital conflict, financial troubles, and social and job pressures can be stressful. Whether the dilemma is real or imagined, the anxiety and effect are quite the same. Certain individuals and professions are more prone to stress than others. A-type personalities (people who are accustomed to running the show) may lock horns with other aggressive individuals while frustrating the more passive B-types whom they may attempt to dominate. People with health problems often have reduced resistance or sensitivity to certain personality types, situations, or environments; it's hard to be patient and understanding when you're not feeling well. A condition as simple as acute hearing can cause extreme irritation in a noisy environment.

High and unreasonable expectations of ourselves are also stressful. Many of our own expectations are based on our perception of what is expected of us by our families, teachers, and mentors.

> There is more to life than increasing its speed.
> —Mohandas Gandhi

The more stressful the profession, the stronger the need for activities that distract and offer respite from the tension. In school and college, students are encouraged to break the routine of study and exams with recreational activities like sports and clubs. Although these activities may promote their own form of competition, they can also offer periods of recovery.

Once we enter the workforce, build families, and acquire additional responsibilities, our recreational time is greatly reduced. The only way to include activities like racquetball, jogging, weight-lifting, golf, fishing, books, movies, chess, mah-jongg, or just getting together with friends into our schedule is to plan and stick to them like other important appointments. If your leisure time is precious, guard and use it well.

The Consequences of Stress

> Every cause produces more than one effect.
> —Herbert Spencer

An occasional burst of adrenalin can serve to motivate and energize us by initiating action or renewed effort. However, continued or frequent stress may cause a number of health- and life-threatening illnesses. Other results of ongoing stress—depression, antisocial behavior, and suicide—are equally well documented.

Depression ranges from occasional moodiness to utter despair. It is a downward spiral that leaches away our energy, motivation, and interest in the issues that affect our careers, personal lives, and health. It builds a wall of indifference that insulates us from the things and people we used to care about. It can lead to job and career failure, divorce, illness, or suicide. Robert Wright ("The Evolution of Despair," *Time*, August 28, 1995) tells us that depression rates in certain industrial nations have been doubling just about every decade.

The physical and psychological conditions caused by stress may also breed or contribute to irritability, impatience, and hostility. Our business and personal relationships suffer as we alienate colleagues, friends, and loved ones with abrupt behavior, rudeness, indifference, or even violence. Wright also points out that "Suicide is the third most common cause of death among young adults in North America" (auto accidents are in first place, followed by homicide).

Managing Stress

> They're rioting in Africa,
> They're starving in Spain;
> There's hurricanes in Florida,
> And Texas needs rain ...
> —(from an old Tom Lehrer song)

Aside from physical confrontation, most stress is brought about by indecision as to how to resolve a perceived problem or threat. The first operative word is *perceived,* since the anxiety is contained within your mind—no matter what the situation, if you're not worried about it, it isn't stressful to you. The second word is *indecision,* because deciding on and enacting a course of action tends to reduce anxiety and the resulting stress.

Stress almost never goes away when left alone. Some issues are easily resolved if dealt with right away, while others demand serious attention. Simple problems may evolve into major dilemmas if ignored ...eventually you'll have to face them, so why not do so early on, before they get much worse? Stress can be brought about by situations that actually occur or that are implied in the form of criticism.

Coping with Criticism

> Only the mediocre are always at their best.
> —Jean Giraudoux

People criticize with the best and worst of intentions. Ironically, the value of criticism is often unrelated to intent: Ill-meaning people may raise valid points, while those who truly wish to help may miss the point entirely. Criticism can be a valuable resource in anticipating and correcting problems, as well as a barometer of how we are being perceived by others.

The trick is to respond to criticism without a feeling of personal threat. Focus on the facts: What happened, why did it happen, what are the ramifications, what can be done to remedy them, and how can it be avoided in the future? Try to detach yourself in your mind's eye as just another player in the mix.

> Learn to accept being wrong without suffering.
> —Dr. Martin Groder

Dr. Groder, a psychiatrist and business consultant in Chapel Hill, North Carolina, advises us to resist the urge to defend ourselves when we are being criticized. For one thing, it's worth encouraging people to offer you criticism (as opposed to stabbing you in the back). Another point to consider is that if one individual perceives you to be at fault, it's a good bet that others may, as well. In most cases you'll earn more respect by accepting your responsibility than by trying to duck it. Either way, facing criticism early is likely to be less stressful in the long run.

Coping with Crises

> Great emergencies and crises show us how much greater our vital resources are than we had supposed.
> —William James

It is a rare individual whose performance at work is unaffected by serious personal problems. An ailing spouse or child, the threat or reality of a divorce, and severe financial loss or obligation can bewilder and incapacitate the best of us. If you are overwhelmed by your predicament, seek help. Emotion is a natural reaction to stress but a handicap in seeking to resolve it. Rational thought can often lead to a practical solution, or at least a realistic perspective on your options. Try to find someone who is willing and qualified to help you through your period of crisis. Many people seek advice and support from close friends, family members, religious advisers, and professional counselors. Often it helps just to have someone to talk to who will listen without criticizing or judging.

Dealing with Divorce

> We must all hang together, or assuredly we shall all hang separately.
> —Benjamin Franklin

Divorce can be as emotionally draining as any other psychological or physical trouble, although there is less tolerance for it as an excuse for poor performance on the job. There are laws that require an employer to grant you time off for certain types of emergencies and illnesses, but they do not pertain to divorce.

Barbara Mende ("Managing Your Career During a Divorce," *National Business Employment Weekly,* October 15-21, 1995) advises against discussing the details of a divorce with people at work.

Limit whatever information you offer to a need-to-know basis. For example, you might tell your boss that you are involved in a divorce proceeding and the extent to which the legal requirements may interfere with your job.

Divorce counselors, attorneys, and participants emphasize the need to separate divorce proceedings from your work life. They also acknowledge that this is difficult to do when heavy demands and concessions are being negotiated that will affect your quality of life for a long time to come. Physical exercise, social activities, and at least one confidant to whom you can express your feelings are a must. The absence of a safety valve can damage both your health and your career.

Mistakes.   Chapter 10 emphasizes the principle of learning from the mistakes you (and others) make so as to improve your future performance. Like criticism, mistakes must first be accepted and recognized for what they are. Once you have embarked upon a plan of action to correct a mistake, or at least drawn from it a valuable lesson for the future, your stress is likely to diminish significantly.

Perspective.   Whatever your problems, they could probably be worse. Sometimes it helps to put the things that trouble us into an entirely different perspective in order to see them with a fresh eye. Like the college student who wrote home:

> Dear Dad,
> Sorry not to have written sooner, but they didn't have any stationery in the hospital. I'm trying to get my marriage annulled—sorry I forgot to tell you about the marriage—but the lawyers say it's hard to do after pregnancy.
> P.S.
> Only kidding about all of the above, but I *did* get two C's and three D's.
> Love, Fred

The Tactics of Good Health

> ..nobody can be in good health if he does not have all the time fresh air, sunshine, and good water.
> —(Oglala Sioux chief) Flying Hawk

Taking an active role in the improvement and maintenance of your health is absolutely essential to your life and, incidentally, your career. Stanford University School of Medicine Dr. Kenneth Pelletier (*Bottom Line*, April 15, 1995) finds that prominent and accomplished men and women do a better job of managing health risks than "typical Americans." Dr. Pelletier believes this is because "[T]hey have had more experience than most people at sustaining a positive attitude when faced with professional and emotional challenges." He contends that this level of control "..comes in part from being brutally honest with themselves."

Self-Control. Lord Nelson, the English naval hero who destroyed Napoleon's naval fleet, suffered from seasickness throughout his life. Somehow, for the sake of country and career, he managed to control this debilitating problem. Self-control is needed to overcome unwanted temptations and to keep to a difficult course. Maintaining a proper diet, avoiding cigarettes and excessive alcohol consumption, and exercising regularly are a natural way of life for some people—and a sacrifice for others. A sustained effort isn't always easy; like most worthwhile pursuits, the achievement of good health may take a lot of effort; fortunately, it can also produce enormous satisfaction.

Habit

> Never give way to melancholy; resist it steadily, for the habit will encroach.
> —Sydney Smith

Much of what we do, both good and bad, is the result of habit. Many good habits can be improved and bad ones changed. Sure, it takes an effort; but if drug, alcohol, and tobacco addicts can break their habits, so can you—if you really want to. When the going gets tough, just think of what's at stake.

An overlooked effect of habit is boredom, which stems from jobs that do not challenge, expectations that remain unfulfilled, and a lack of activity. Ernie J. Zelinski (*The Joy of Not Working*) proposes "..taking antiboredom steps—like searching for ways to make a job more interesting or trying to get promoted .." to help relieve the boredom. It can also be a good idea to review your goals and recent progress. New or redefined ambitions, and formulating an active game plan toward achieving them, are anything but boring.

Health Problems

> We live, not as we wish to, but as we can.
> —Menander

▼▼▼

Anyone who doesn't know about healthy foods, diets, and exercise just isn't paying attention.

> Nothing succeeds like excess.
> —Oscar Wilde

Detective Lou Scarcetta, of Brooklyn's North Homicide Squad, has many stories to tell. The one he told to us was of patrolman Grady.

"When he left the Marine Corps in the 70s, Grady weighed a trim 180 pounds. Irregular hours and good food elevated his weight to 205, but that wasn't a problem, since most of it was muscle. Over the years, however, Grady worked himself up to sergeant and, via Nathan's Famous (hot dogs), Kashas Famous Pabok, and dozens of other restaurants, over 300 pounds. No longer able to stand a foot patrol, Grady was assigned to a series of desk and sedentary posts until being reassigned to another precinct. There he became a Sergeant on Patrol, until his burgeoning bulk destroyed the seats in three radio cars.

"A new assignment to a plainclothes anticrime unit didn't work out, since Grady couldn't even walk after street muggers, much less run after them. So they let him supervise street crime from unmarked cars, until he broke a few more seats. Once he fell asleep along the highway on his way home, and when a patrolman woke him up, Grady couldn't get his police shield out of his pocket to identify himself.

"Back to desk work, in charge of the 4 A.M. to 12 shift, alas, Grady couldn't manage to stay awake due to the lack of oxygen to his heart. He tried a number of diets but by now his body couldn't respond, and he had to retire from the police force at the age of 42."

The use of drugs and alcohol to deal with stress is a crutch with side-effects. In many cases, a dependency on even prescription medications can be as harmful as using the unlawful kinds. Over time, they mask the symptoms and discourage facing up to underlying causes.

Health Maintenance

> A man's own observation, what he finds good of and what he finds hurt of, is the best physic to preserve health.
> —Francis Bacon

The best way to deal with health problems is and always has been to avoid them in the first place. This is done by pursuing a healthy life, i.e., eating properly, getting enough rest, and seeking the assistance of medical professionals when something is or appears to be wrong (before it gets any worse). Regular physical examinations are a must to diagnose potential disorders early on. Physical and other types of illness, like depression and abnormally aggressive behavior, both need to be taken seriously and treated by a qualified professional.

Dr. Isadore Rosenfeld, Cornell Medical Center (*Doctor, What Should I Eat?*), identifies the health problems that he most frequently encounters in his practice and the ways to help prevent them through proper diet. These diseases include arteriosclerosis, cancer, and high blood pressure (hypertension); his dietary recommendations are to reduce intake of saturated and polyunsaturated fats, foods high in cholesterol, salt, nitrate- or salt-cured foods, and alcohol; and to increase consumption of vegetables, fruits, and nonfat or low-fat milk products in order to get enough betacarotene, vitamins C and E (antioxidants), potassium, calcium, and magnesium. Of course, individual requirements vary according to our health, activities, age, and other factors.

Smoking is no longer socially desirable among adults, and cigarette advertising has been largely curtailed. Most companies in North America and other industrialized nations have eliminated smoking from their premises. With all the irrefutable information available on the disastrous effects of smoking on one's health, it is a wonder that so many people continue to do it.

A healthy body is the ideal host for a healthy mind. When we're very young, many of us take our health for granted. As we mature, our bodies need increasingly more attention. Millions of men and women use regular exercise to maintain their fitness; health clubs, exercise machines, videos, and classes are marketed extensively throughout the electronic and paper media. We all know about the advantages of cardiovascular and other fitness activities, and still the majority of people over 30 get little if any exercise. It's a question of priorities and scheduling: If you recognize the need, you do it; if not, you don't.

CAREER BUSTER 9

IF YOUR PRIORITIES ARE OUT OF SYNCH, SO IS YOUR CAREER

> You can never get enough of what you don't really want.
> —Eric Hoffer

Without clear objectives, people meander through their days, careers, and lives as aimlessly as tumbleweed out on the prairie, borne along by wind, routine, and chance. Purpose focuses energy and resources; destinations provide direction and a sense of accomplishment when reached. And when your long- and short-term goals have been defined, you need priorities to sort through, organize, and pursue them.

Goals are based on values; priorities are the order of importance we assign to goals, the sequence in which we intend to achieve them. These are not to be confused with routines, like those that bring you to and home from work each day. Habit patterns require no particular goal, other than earning a living—even sheep know how to leave the barn when it is time to graze. But sheep have no say about the use to which their fleece is put, nor do they complain of boredom, frustration, or regret.

> You've got to be very careful if you don't know where
> you're going, because you may not get there.
> —Yogi Berra

There are many playful variations on this theme. At first glance, they may seem to be frivolous word games unworthy of serious attention. The idea that we might not have a clear picture of our objectives is uncomfortable, unsettling, annoying. Indeed, some of us really do have well-prioritized goals, although even these are worth reviewing and updating from time to time. Those who aren't quite so sure may find this the most challenging career buster of all, and the most meaningful to overcome.

CAREER SAVERS

The Art of Establishing Priorities
Choosing a Career
The Tactics of Pursuing Objectives

The Art of Establishing Priorities

> The quest for success always begins with a target.
> —Tom Morris

Everybody needs a life philosophy, a reason for living as we do. Our motivations are bordered by the rules of behavior to which we adhere—a sense of right and wrong—and marked by our individual style. These help us to select our goals, establish our priorities, and achieve them. Goals are the standards by which we measure our progress. Priorities are the order of importance we assign to goals. When our goals have been defined and prioritized, they become objectives.

Defining Goals

> Goals should be specific, realistic, and measurable.
> —William Dyer

People rarely rise above the level of their goals. Setting goals too low inclines us to underachieve and become satisfied with less than we are capable of, while setting them too high can be self-defeating and discouraging. We need to find a balance that stretches our limits without causing us to burn out or fall too far short of our ability.

Goals need to be *specific,* realistically *attainable,* and in some way *measurable* in order to be meaningful. To write a book is not a goal; finishing two chapters a month is a goal. In order to achieve this, you need to develop an action plan (number of chapters, schedules and deadlines, time and resources needed to research and write each chapter, and so on) and then to implement your plan.

Having a Purpose

> The primary motivation in human behavior is the desire
> to avoid pain.

To achieve worthwhile results you need to have a specific purpose in mind. It isn't enough to *want* to do something even for the best of reasons: If you don't go about it in the right way, you can still lose out.

Before choosing and defining your objectives, you need a clear idea of what you want to accomplish. This means differentiating between "fuzzy" goals (e.g., to retire in a house in the country, sooner or later) and specific goals (to buy a house in the country in the beginning of 2001 and retire before the end of that year). Specific goals are linked to periods of time and plans to accomplish them. In order to buy that house in the country in 2001, you'll need to decide by then on one or more possible locations, project what the houses in these areas are likely to be selling for toward the end of the year 2000, and figure out how to pay for it.

> The desire for posessions is rarely satisfied through acquisition.

The urge to acquire things and privileges is the driving force behind a good deal of human activity and the cause of enormous frustration. Wanting more than we own is encouraged by the media and peer-group competition, an illusion that suggests we will feel good about ourselves by buying certain objects and services.

> To be is to do.
> —Albert Camus

John is a recent "graduate" of the Florida prison system. He has served time for a number of nonviolent crimes, including shoplifting, car theft, and credit card fraud. He is now enrolled in a community college computer program and appears headed for a career in data processing. John told us, "I always wanted to be somebody—but I could never figure out *who* I wanted to be. Well, this psychologist who used to come to see me every week, she made me realize that I already *was* somebody, in fact, had been all my life.

"At first, I didn't want to talk to her, because I figured, I'm not crazy or anything like that, just unlucky, so why should I be talking to a shrink? But after a while, she convinced me that it wasn't her job to cure crazy people, just to help normal people like me who have problems. Well, she helped me to discover who I was and what I liked and didn't like about myself, and then I used the good qualities as a base to start changing the ideas and habits that were getting me into trouble. You know," he admitted, "it's damned humiliating to have to admit to yourself that you've been a jerk all your life, until you realize that you've got a lot of company. And now, for the first time in my life, I've got a real goal, which is not only to stay out of jail, but to prove to myself and to Miriam—the psychologist—that I'm not a jerk anymore."

To do is to be.
—Jean-Paul Sartre

Napoleon Hill's first (of seventeen) principles of success is to develop a single, or principle, goal. Hill prescribes that you describe in your mind a definite image of what you want, and then write it down; decide what you're willing to sacrifice in exchange for your goal; set a specific date for achieving it; establish a plan for getting it done; put it into action right away! Create a written statement of these steps and be prepared to review and revise them daily, or as often as needed. Check regularly to see if you're on the right track, and do your best not to deviate from your determined path.

Paying the Price. Every goal exacts a cost in terms of sacrifice (what you must give up in order to pursue it) and result (what you pay if you achieve it, e.g., increased competition, responsibility, and tension). Consider the likely consequences of your potential goals (Chapter 17), and reconsider those you may not be willing to accept. Jogging every morning may mean going to bed earlier or doing with less sleep; if you become the department head, how much will that change your relationship with your (former) colleagues?

Both success and failure take a toll. The victory that costs too much is hollow and short-lived; the loss that discourages renewed effort is utter defeat. Before making promises or pursuing objectives that will have a major impact on other people, consider the price you'll have to pay for your success... or failure. If you're convinced that the expense of winning is justified, what about the potential downside? Can you survive the cost of losing?

The Wrong Stuff

> He set his heart upon the goal, not on the prize.
> —William Watson

Success and failure are labels based on predetermined standards and results. It is difficult to succeed at someone else's goal, and even harder to enjoy it.

> Do not seek to follow in the footsteps of the men of old;
> seek what they sought.
> —Matsuo Basho

If your goals were formed before you completed your teen years, be sure that they are truly yours. When someone else—parents, teachers, peer-group members whom you respect and admire—suggests a direction for you, review it to determine if it fits. Is this what you want to be and do? Does it conform to your abilities? Is it something you enjoy? Does it *feel* right?

Prioritizing

> We make choices throughout our lives about how to spend our time, and we spend most of our remaining time living with the consequences of these choices.

High achievers rely on carefully detailed priorities. Without priorities, it is possible to work hard for many years without getting any closer to your goals. The first step is to evaluate activities and tasks in order to decide which ones are worth doing. Then you need to rate your to-do lists by importance and urgency: How crucial is the issue, and when must it be done?

> Putting first things first is an issue at the very heart of life.
> —Stephen Covey

The choices we must make concerning what to do first, later, or never have to be made in order to get anything done. They are complicated by the fact that not all decisions are between *good* and *bad* alternatives, but rather good vs better, poor vs worse, and shades of gray that can be difficult to judge. It is sobering to consider that instinctive, quickly-made decisions—or indecisions—can cause so many consequences down the road.

When you prioritize a task, consider the following criteria:

Requirement: Is this something I must do?

Goal-fulfillment: To what goal(s) will it contribute?

Deadline: Is there an impending deadline, and if so, when is it?

Effort: How difficult is it? Will it require a major effort/additional resources?

Consequences: What is likely to happen if I do/don't do it?

▼▼▼

If it isn't a requirement, doesn't contribute to a significant goal, has no impending deadline, will not demand a particular effort, won't benefit you in any meaningful way, and isn't likely to cause you trouble if you decide not to do it, then it probably isn't a major priority. If it's something you absolutely have to do but can put off for five or six months without any negative consequences, it may be a major but not necessarily an immediate priority. On the other hand, suppose you need to organize a project that isn't due for several weeks but will involve the participation of a number of people: Even if it isn't a high priority in terms of importance, time constraints may push it to the top of your urgency list.

> He listens well who takes notes.
> —Dante

Adventurous and indifferent people trust their priorities to memory; others write themselves notes on scraps of paper, post-its, or in their calendar books; most successful individuals create detailed lists. You may find it convenient to organize your priorities by importance (impact), urgency (available time), or both:

Importance

ITEM	PURPOSE	DEADLINE	EFFORT: PEOPLE/DAYS	!!	ACTION
Config. report	status/ schedule	12/30	JD:5/Pete:5/ me: 2	A	—get their input —review status —finish writing —have BW review
budget	reg. (must)	11/1	me/3 more	A	—final.sales $$ —see BW —justify new acct
hire jr. acct	increased workload	after budget	Pete & I interview	B	—justify —write require. —*check w/BW* —tell HR
write up requirements for jr. acct	—convince BW —HR	open	Pete: 2 hrs/ me: 1 hr	B	—tell Pete

Urgency

ITEM	PURPOSE	DEADLINE	EFFORT: PEOPLE/DAYS	ACTION
meeting with Config. team	establish deadlines	10:AM today	TBD	prepare questions & guidelines
cleaners	pick up/ drop off	6:PM today	me	leave by 5:15 *latest*
flowers for secretary	birthday	tomorrow 12/11	me	call early in morn.
Config. report	status/ schedule	12/30	JD/Pete/me 5/5/2	check status

When creating a schedule, focus on priorities rather than items. Since your lists are only as good as they are current, they must be updated, edited, and added to on an ongoing basis.

Keep commitments to yourself and to others. Strive to balance flexiblity with persistence. Keep people (leadership issues) first and things (management issues) second. Consider the goal to be accomplished; the way you'd like to achieve it; the available resources; standards of measurability; potential consequences, i.e., the relationship between rewards and performance. Focus upon *solving* a particular problem, and *coping* with a major problem until you're able to resolve it (by solving the little problems of which it is comprised). When you face a complicated issue, begin by developing a purpose (direction) rather than a fixed objective to be accomplished. If you keep chopping away with a sharp axe, in time the mighty oak will fall.

Updating Priorities

> It is profitable Wisdom to know when we have done
> enough.
> —William Penn

As conditions change, your goals and your priorities need to evolve accordingly. What you wanted a year ago, even last month, may no longer seem as pertinent today; often, goals that have been fairly well achieved fall in importance to new or (formerly) lesser ones. As you grow, your expectations may expand, and your perception of the circumstances that influence your career can alter drastically. Review your priorities, consider alternatives, check your progress, and try to keep your balance.

Choosing a Career

Shortly before (former British prime minister) Margaret Thatcher graduated from university, she was discussing politics with a group of young people at a village dance. When someone remarked, "What you really want to do is be an MP (member of Parliament), isn't it?" "Almost without thinking," reminisces Thatcher, "I said, 'yes, that really is what I want to do.' ..When I went to bed that night I found that I had a lot on my mind." (*The Path to Power*, by Margaret Thatcher).

Some people seem to know what they want to be when they "grow up" while still in grade school; others discover career directions during high school or college. If they choose careers that suit their talents and continue to inspire their efforts and interest, they are indeed fortunate.

The advantages of making an early career choice are being able to study, practice, and develop experience and a reputation in your field. This is particularly valuable in the highly specialized professions. The longer you wait, the more difficult it will be to break into singing, medicine, and astrophysics; the earlier you begin selling services like insurance, the sooner you will be able to develop a profitable client base.

Fashion designer Catherine Huang never doubted that she was going to be a fashion designer. She "..realized that the academic subjects I studied in school would enrich my life in literature, the arts, and in practical matters, like balancing a checkbook and purchasing a house, but fashion design was my objective." Catherine graduated from the Los Angeles Fashion Institute, took an entry-level job, and worked her way up through several West Coast, Chicago, and New York City fashion houses. She is currently the head designer for a well-known New York City company.

The downside of making an early career choice is growing bored, dead-ending, or burning out (Chapter 13). It can be difficult for a 40-year-old to live with a decision made in his or her teens. Also, certain professions periodically fade from favor while others may blossom. Some of us are late bloomers and don't find ourselves until later in life. We may not know what holds our interest, or at what we are best suited, until we've had a chance to experience a number of alternatives. A close friend of ours drifted through careers in teaching, translating, educational publishing, and computer systems before evolving into his vocation as a writer. "I needed to achieve success at other things," he confided, "to gain the confidence and courage to face the possibility of failing at my ultimate objective."

Too many people never make and pursue a conscious career decision, but rather follow patterns in which—through family affiliations, social connections, or just blind circumstances—they find themselves ensconced. If you are a procrastinator, you need to come to terms with the fact that this trait is holding you back. Divide your goals into bite-sized portions, and schedule them on specific dates. Force yourself to get them done on schedule .. this is a realistic way to try to reprogram yourself to be more productive. Reward yourself for even small achievements. And focus upon doing a good job without requiring a perfect result.

The Tactics of Pursuing Objectives

Where You Are.   To get from here to there, you've got to know where *here* is. This axiom is the essence of all progress. Assuming that you know exactly where you are just because you're there is naive. In order to move up, outward, or toward a specific goal, you need a solid base from which to launch yourself in the right direction.

Where You Want to Be

> He who determines the end, provides the means.
> —Benedetto Varchi

Your goal is where you want to be. Practically speaking, it should be attainable or all of your efforts will be wasted. Not everyone is qualified to model swimsuits, earn a living playing poker, or direct a large corporation. More realistic goals might be to run for office in your civic club, work at getting and staying fit, or manage your department.

Getting There

> A journey of a thousand miles begins with a single step.
> —Chinese Proverb

Like problems, major quests need to be broken down and pursued by smaller portions. Every significant journey requires careful planning, selection, assessment of progress, and continual focus upon the objective.

No matter what your goal, there's no substitute for proper preparation (Chapter 21). Pursuing a career objective is like planning a challenging journey with maps, logistics, and personal components factored in. Reaching your goal means having a clear image of your destination and assembling the tools and materials you will need along the way. The early pioneers relied on horse-drawn wagons to carry them, scouts to guide their way, dried foodstocks to sustain them, guns to supplement their diet and provide protection, and a good deal of hope, luck, and sheer determination. They found land on which to build their homes and futures. Columbus, who was looking for a passageway to the Orient, found America instead.

The 80/20 axiom can help you sort through the bulk of possible activities. This principle suggests that 80% of the things that benefit you are derived from 20% of what you spend your time and efforts doing. For example, 20% of your clients generate 80% of your business, and 20% of your employees account for 80% of your productivity. These numbers are only approximate, but in practice they signify that a small and select portion of your resources will produce the bulk of your meaningful accomplishments.

> There's a reason why God gave us two ears and one mouth.
> —J.B. Fuqua

Thomas A. Edison defined the first requisite for success as "The ability to apply your physical and mental energies to one problem incessantly without growing weary." (*Success Magazine*, February, 1898, and reprinted in 1991.) The key to focusing is to maximize attention on a specific issue without getting sidetracked or reacting immediately. The more you say, the less you hear, and the less others will contribute.

> "People enjoy listening to a good speaker, although they may be intimidated to offer their ideas immediately afterwards," says communications consultant Robin Chin of Singapore. "When you just listen and appear to focus on what they're saying, they tend to be flattered and encouraged to offer you more information."

> I find the great thing in this world is not so much where we stand, as in what direction we are moving.
> —Oliver Wendell Holmes

The road to a career objective is laden with detours, trenches, and alternate paths. The final part of the trip is the voyage itself, the act of getting from where you are to where you'd like to be. Since people are motivated differently, we can't all use exactly the same path or fuel. Some of us are able to decide upon a direction and move steadily toward it without wavering; others need encouragement and rest stops (smaller goals) along the way.

The Right Stuff

> Whatever is worth doing at all, is worth doing well.
> —Philip Dormer Stanhope

Pursuing major objectives depends upon an accurate awareness of yourself and your environment. Even if you know what you want and have a plan for getting it, you've got to want it strongly enough to maintain a sustained effort. Consistency, tenacity, and patience are all part of the commitment fueled by a passion to succeed.

> Jackie Robinson knew what he was in for when he set out to break the color barrier in professional baseball. Once he had become a member of the Brooklyn Dodgers, his objective was to help create an atmosphere that would make it possible for other blacks to join the major leagues. This meant putting up with enormous abuse from the public, the media, and his peers, few of whom were as intelligent, much less as talented, as he was. Jackie's historical success required substantial baseball skills, vast reserves of enthusiasm for his cause, personal commitment, and perseverance. He had to maintain a consistent level of behavior in the face of great indignity.

Few of us encounter obstacles of this nature in our lifetimes, but there are challenges enough for everyone. Degrees of difficulty vary according to the magnitude of—and your proximity to—your objectives. The longer and tougher the journey, the more of the right stuff you need to get there.

> It's not our lack of knowledge that often makes us act wrong, it's our arrogance.
> —Vartan Gregorian

To achieve a goal you need a clear and realistic understanding of your abilities and the circumstances relating to your goal. What level of experience, skills, political contacts, time, effort, and resources is it likely to take? Be honest and realistic with yourself: If special talents that you lack are needed, what are your chances for success? If nepotism, sexism, or some other physical barrier stands in your way, you will have an uphill battle. If years of experience are needed, you may have to construct a ladder of objectives to move you in the right direction.

> She: *Explain the difference between* ignorance *and*
>   indifference.
> He: *I don't know and I don't care.*

Enthusiasm is the fuel that powers all ambition and sustained effort. Indifference is a façade, a screen to hide behind, a rationalization for not trying. Without enthusiasm, it is difficult to convince yourself—and those around you—that you are capable of achieving your goal.

> The strongest of all warriors are these two: Time and
> Patience.
> —Leo Tolstoi

Composure is the counterpart of enthusiasm, the glue that holds together the pursuit of your objectives. Patience keeps you from making hasty decisions, allows you to time your efforts to maximum advantage, and to sustain your effort. Without patience, little that is worthy of your time and effort will ever be accomplished.

> To tend, unfailingly, unflinchingly, toward a goal, is the
> secret of success.
> —Anna Pavlova (Russian ballerina)

A strong commitment is needed to direct your flow of energy along the right path and to sustain a prolonged effort. You don't become a skilled psychologist, manager, or sculptor on ability alone. You've got to develop your abilities with study, practice, and dedication to your goal. Otherwise you drop into the pool of talented underachievers who live in envy of those who were willing to make the effort.

> The secret of success is consistency to purpose.
> —Benjamin Disraeli

Consistency is a form of agreement, a harmony with what has occurred in the past, a compatibility of purpose and of action. Consistency applies both to your objectives and your means of achieving them. This is not the same as stubbornness, which implies a lack of willingness to grow and change, but rather a constructive and cohesive pattern on which you, and those around you, can rely.

The story of Daniel Ruettiger, hero of the movie, *Rudy*, is one of commitment to an unlikely goal and tenacity in achieving it. Rudy's objective was to play football at the University of Notre Dame. His first problem was that his high school grades weren't up to Notre Dame's admission requirements; if that wasn't enough, Rudy stood only five feet six and weighed about 185 pounds—hardly major college football stature. So he took his friends' advice, at first, and settled for a job at a local power plant.

But Rudy's obsession continued to haunt him through two years on the job and two more in the Navy. After a short return to the power plant, he quit his job and enrolled in a small junior college located right across the street from Notre Dame and well within sight of the Golden Dome that represented his objective. Rudy dedicated himself to raising his grades, and after two years he succeeded in enrolling in the University of Notre Dame. He used his boundless enthusiasm to talk his way onto the "scout" team, a group that helped the varsity prepare for their regular opponents. Still another two years passed, and the final home game of Rudy's senior year arrived. This would be his last chance to bring his dream to life.

Fortunately for Rudy, a number of his teammates prevailed upon the coach to allow him to dress for the game in a varsity uniform. Late in the final quarter, with Notre Dame comfortably ahead of their opponent, the fans (who had learned of Rudy's story) began to chant: "We want Rudy, we want Rudy." The coach relented and sent Rudy onto the field with less than a minute of time remaining in the game. At the age of twenty-seven, Rudy cashed in twenty-seven seconds of his impossible dream.

The moral to this story is that if you want something strongly enough and are willing to pay the price, you just may get it ..and they may even make a movie about you in the bargain.

On the other hand, pursuing what is not conceivably attainable is a waste of time and energy. *Reaching for the stars* encourages us to stretch ourselves to the limits of our potential. It doesn't mean that we should set the unattainable as goals. Being the very best you can at what you do is certainly realistic. With some talent and a lot of work and dedication, you might become your company's top accountant, engineer, or plumber. The important thing is to decide for yourself what is important to you, and to reconcile your goals with the reality of the options that are open to you.

Don't Let Up After Achieving—or Failing to Achieve—a Goal

> Okay, we've won. What do we do now?
> —(Canadian prime minister) Brian Mulroney (in 1988)

Things that aren't going well tend to receive the bulk of our attention. However, there are two important reasons for paying at least some attention to our areas of least concern: first, because most things could work better than they do; second, to keep them from deteriorating into problems. In a world where all available knowl-edge doubles every five years, conditions change from day to day, and yesterday's solution may not apply to tomorrow's needs. Problems are much easier to fix before they happen, and momentum is more easily maintained than initiated.

> Those who know how to win are much more numerous than those who know how to make proper use of their victories.
> —Polybius

Inertia and gravity are fundamental laws by which the universe and all its creatures function. In pursuing our objectives, these principles equate to habit: We tend to keep moving along a familiar path, and we have trouble getting started in a new direction. We all need some inertia—habit patterns—to function normally, although we may have to adjust old habits in order to grow or change direction (Chapter 12). It's a question of balance: Too much inertia and you can't lift yourself out of a rut, too little and you'll have to learn to brush your teeth all over again each morning. If you're moving in the wrong (or not the best) direction, you may need to redirect your efforts.

A goal is not an end unto itself, but a step toward the fulfill-ment of ongoing objectives. While you are encouraged to enjoy and reward yourself for the achievement of a major goal, beware the trap of letting up. Victory creates momentum which, if not maintained, fades into nostalgia. Attaining an objective is a milestone; the greater the accomplishment, the more important it becomes for you to re-assess your goals, redefine objectives, refine your plans, and renew your efforts. Use each achievement to propel you forward; turn the energy into motion; step up to the next level.

CAREER BUSTER 10

FAILING TO LEARN FROM MISTAKES
MAY CAUSE YOU TO REPEAT THEM

When you have faults, do not fear to abandon them.
—Confucius

Mistakes are errors in opinion, understanding, or judgment, such as when we do something wrong or fail to do it right. A fault can also be an error or a responsibility for something that went wrong. More commonly we think of faults as imperfections, such as a lack of certain desirable qualities. In this chapter, we view mistakes and faults as errors that can be recognized and, hopefully, improved upon.

The cliché that everybody makes mistakes is little comfort when things are going wrong. While it is human to err, we must live with our mistakes and deal with their consequences. The first step toward reducing the mistakes we make is to acknowledge that we make them. But there is a natural reluctance toward self-criticism, a tendency to protect ourselves with rationalizations like, "It wasn't really my fault," and "I'm only human." The trick is to view our errors as activities like hitting a golf ball or learning to speak a foreign language: sometimes good, sometimes not so good, but always subject to improvement.

Reducing errors takes an honest effort .. sometimes it requires coming to terms with unpleasant realities about ourselves. In the long run, however, this may be less demanding than continuing to swim upstream. The best part is that it isn't absolutely necessary to make mistakes in order to learn from them, for we can also learn from those that other people make.

CAREER SAVERS

The Art of Recognition
The Tactics of Mistakes

The Art of Recognition

> Intelligence is learning from your own mistakes; wisdom
> is learning from those of other people.
> —Ruhtra

The most vivid lessons are derived from our worst mistakes and those of people close to us. As these experiences can be emotionally challenging, it may be difficult to recognize them objectively: I messed up by doing this or failing to do that. Why was it wrong? What were my alternatives? Why did I do it this way instead of that way? And how can I work toward doing a better job next time? It's easier to identify mistakes in which we are uninvolved. However, it can be more difficult to learn from them because we may not believe that they apply to us. The key is to recognize the parallels between what we see other people do and our own actions.

Accepting Responsibility

> The greatest of faults, I should say, is to be conscious of
> none.
> —Thomas Carlyle

Before learning from a mistake, you must first acknowledge that it *is* a mistake. While some of our miscues are obvious to us, others may be open to interpretation: short-term loss vs long-term gain, someone else's fault, factors out of our control, and so on. One thing is certain: You cannot fix a problem, much less reverse a negative pattern, until you (1) recognize that it is a problem, and (2) realistically accept your role and responsibility in its occurrence. This means owning up to the fact that you did something wrong, and it may also involve admitting it to others.

One way to recognize a mistake is when it's brought to your attention. When you are blamed for doing something wrong, then the perception of a fault exists. Even if the accusation is unfair and the error was caused by someone else, you may still need to deal with the situation. If you can resolve it with a credible explanation, so much the better. Be careful, though, to avoid creating the impression that you are making excuses and trying to cover yourself. Don't say:

- That was Charlie's fault, not mine.
- Why am I always getting blamed for things that aren't my fault?

Do say:

- As a matter of fact, I was not involved in making that decision.
- For the record, I was brought into the picture after that particular problem surfaced.

If you *were* even partially to blame, accept your responsibility in a gracious and positive manner. Don't say:

- We were well aware of the issue before you pointed it out.
- Haven't you got better things to do than criticize?

Do say:

- You're right about that, although we're back on track now.
- Thank you for pointing this out to me. I'll look into it right away.

Cleo Thomas, President of an Orange, Connecticut manufacturing firm, thinks that people who take responsibility for their actions are no longer rewarded or acknowledged by society: "People believe that it is acceptable to shift the blame for their mistakes to other people or circumstances." This practice is transparent in business and other workplace environments, for it is difficult to fool your colleagues for very long. Eventually you earn a reputation as a responsible individual or a buck-passing BS artist. And once the latter reputation has taken hold, it's hard to change.

The Tactics of Mistakes

> ..the wise men shun the mistakes of fools, but fools do not imitate the successes of the wise.
> —Marcus Porcius Cato (the Elder)

Mistakes are inevitable and an important part of the learning process, if we choose to profit from them.

Learning from the Mistakes of Others

> Draw from others the lesson that may profit yourself.
> —Plubius Terenius Afer

It is easier to recognize other people's mistakes than our own. On the other hand, we may not take them seriously if they do not directly affect us. Try this: Begin by making a list of the kinds of mistakes that you see people make and categorizing them, e.g., bad decisions; poor planning; reacting too quickly/failing to act on time; inconsistency/unwillingness to make changes; poor communication and listening skills; impatience; stubbornness; and so on. Speculate as to why you think these people made these errors. Are they common or unusual? Then ask yourself if you do not, from time to time, make any of these same mistakes. Pretend that you are a close friend or fellow worker, and that you will be paid $100 for every fault you can ascribe to the person who is really you. How many can you come up with?

Learning from Our Own Mistakes

> Experience is the name everyone gives to their mistakes.
> —Oscar Wilde

People who are insecure about their judgment are often reluctant to admit when they are wrong ...even to themselves. The self-security that enables us to face up to our mistakes and learn from them comes, like most good things, with practice.

A simple formula is to ask a few trusted friends, family members, and colleagues to make a list of the kinds of mistakes they've noticed you make, and approximately how often. After you've received lists from at least three or four people, combine and rate the faults as frequent, occasional, or only once or twice. Important: Be sure to include them all—every last one of them—whether you agree or not. Add any additional mistakes that you can think of to the list. When you're done, find a quiet time and place to think about them, beginning with the most frequent. Were you aware of them at the time? Did you acknowledge them? Why do you think they happened? Have you taken any steps to remedy the results of these mistakes? What can you do to reduce, if not eliminate, them in the future?

> The legendary Beardstown Ladies Investment Group makes a point of acknowledging and learning from their mistakes. They've made their share of blunders, such as buying and selling stocks at the wrong time and failing to sell at the right time. Whenever this happens, they investigate exactly what went wrong, and why, so as to avoid making the same mistake in the future. Their ability to profit from their errors has lead to an average return on investments of over 23% since 1983.

Rationalizing

> We confess to little faults only to persuade ourselves that
> we have no great ones.
> —Francois de La Rochefoucauld

Defensive behavior isn't limited to refusing to accept our faults or arguing against them. Most of us are prone to occasional rationalizations whereby we create excuses in which to couch unpleasant facts. The two most popular forms of rationalization are admitting to some minor fault while hiding from ourselves a nastier reality, and excuses that let us at least partially off the hook. These can be neatly combined into something like: "I should never have allowed that argument to get started. Everyone knows what a hothead he is, and it's my fault for having talked to him in the first place." Notice how the speaker accepts responsibility for a minor mistake (talking to that *hothead*) while ascribing the real fault (arguing) to the other guy.

False Assumptions

> There's no such thing as an accidental injury. Every time
> someone gets 'accidentally' injured, someone made a
> mistake. God ain't doing this stuff, we are.
> —(Houston surgeon) James Duke

One of the major reasons for mistakes is making false assumptions. Have you ever been in a situation where your understanding of an issue conflicted with someone else's? Since it is unlikely that you were both right, it is probable that at least one of you was wrong. In other words, the information that you and/or the other person thought of as *knowledge* was merely an *opinion*. Yet you were probably ready to act upon this information because you assumed it to be correct.

> If it doesn't seem right, it probably isn't.

Many of the decisions you make are based on what you hear and observe. The difficulty lies in the fact that our observations are filtered through our own preconceptions, and each of us perceives the same things differently. Trust your instincts: When something doesn't seem to make sense, verify your understanding of the issue by asking questions. Two possibilities to consider are:

1. *You may be misinterpreting the "facts."*
Insufficient or inaccurate information, a bias, or a blind spot can lead you astray. The rule of thumb when all else fails is to *seek consistency*: Does the event you're trying to grasp appear to fit a pattern? Is it consistent with what you have observed and understood previously?

2. *There may be no rational explanation.*
People aren't always aware of what they're doing, much less why. Haven't you ever done anything that you were at a loss to explain even to yourself afterwards? Imagine how difficult it would be for someone else to try to figure you out at times like these.

Habit

> To fall into a habit is to cease to be.
> —Miguel de Unamundo

Momentum is a seductive force. It's so comfortable to continue moving in a familiar direction doing things the way we're used to doing them. Habits can be awfully tough to break even when you want to change them—as addictive as drugs—and equally destructive to a career.

The Consequences

> The physician can bury his mistakes, but the architect can only advise his client to plant vines.
> —Frank Lloyd Wright

The way you deal with the consequences of a mistake has a more lasting impact than the mistake itself. Since all activities have side effects, it is reasonable to expect to have to deal with them from time to time. It is no exaggeration to say that just about everything that happens on our planet displeases *someone;* a positive accomplishment in one place may be seen as a mistake elsewhere. If you face up to the consequences of your actions, it is likely that the credits from your achievements will heavily outweigh the debits of your errors.

Coping

> People who can't cope with failure are not likely to succeed.
> —Dean Keith Simonton, Professor of Psychology,
>   Univ. of California at Davis.

Failure is a temporary state of mind; like success, it can be reversed. The difference between failure and challenge is mostly a matter of attitude: Do you allow your setbacks and misfortunes to push you into a defensive posture, or do you draw from them the knowledge and inspiration to do a better job next time? Do you quit when things go wrong, or do you hang in there and try again? As incredible as it sounds, Michael Jordan was once cut from his high school basketball team.

Elevating Error into Virtue

> When I make a mistake it's a beaut!
> —(former New York City mayor) Fiorello La Guardia

People with troubled pasts have been known to turn their lives around by using their mistakes as launching pads. Reformed felons have become role models to impoverished children by encouraging them to finish school and stay out of trouble. Don Imus, of the popular *Imus in the Morning* radio program, flaunts his past addictions to an adoring national audience, an inspiration by example of a loser who turned himself into a winner.

CAREER BUSTER 11

MIS-FITTING INTO THE CORPORATE CULTURE PUTS YOU ON THE OUTSIDE LOOKING IN

When you are in Rome live in the Roman style ...
—Saint Ambrose

Fitting in is simply a matter of conformity. Conflicts arise when the fit is uncomfortable or unnatural, or when people are unaware of certain aspects of the culture in which they find themselves. To fit in, you need to be mindful of the behaviors by which you are being judged. Then you can decide whether or not the required level of conformity is acceptable to you.

The two most important behavior characteristics in any business environment are courtesy and willingness to learn. These qualities are universally acknowledged in just about every occupation. Firefighters may wear different clothes and do different work from accountants, but rudeness is annoying and unacceptable in both cultures. Whether you are a bank officer or corrections officer, your place of work has a culture you must fit into in order to survive and thrive.

Rich Yorde runs his own business in Gambier, Ohio. His first job out of graduate school was as an instructor in the theater department of a small state university. As Rich puts it, "The faculty, like the cattle (who outnumbered the local residents 3 to 1), were relatively anonymous. Having graduated from a top-rated liberal arts college and studied with a noted theater professional, I was all geared up to do my thing, that is, to challenge students. Isn't that what it's all about?

"The problem derived from the fact that our department's primary mission was to produce F.T.E.'s (full time equivalents), a formula by which the administration evaluated its departments and assigned funding. Youthful idealism kept me from appreciating this little nuance. While the other faculty discussed the merits of offering more F.T.E.'s for non-academic classes like acting and ushering, I remained devoted to preparing our students for the World of Professional Theater. A short time later, the word came down that my teaching performance was in serious question, and that numerous student complaints had been received regarding the arduous academic demands I made on them. My contract was not renewed: I had failed to read the 'corporate' culture and was out of a job."

CAREER SAVERS
The Art of Fitting In
The Tactics of Fitting In

The Art of Fitting In

> To get ahead you have to know your company's system
> and understand how to use it. That's the only way you
> can work within it, through it, or around it.
> —Mark H. McCormack.

Fitting into most work-related environments rarely imposes any unusual demands. A personable smile, an optimistic attitude, and a reasonable sense of humor blend well with most conditions. Observing what your colleagues do and listening to what they say is your best introduction to the culture.

Reading the Handwriting

> Things are never quite what they seem.

Adjusting to and thriving in a corporate or institutional culture requires political awareness, adaptability, and good interpersonal, networking, and teamwork skills. There may be any number of conflicting interests and priorities among your leaders and colleagues. The key is learning what is needed to gain their acceptance and trust, and then doing it successfully. How can you uncover all those hidden agendas? You probably can't; but you can find out which of the policymakers and trendsetters carry the most weight, pay particular attention to their statements and activities, and develop a personal relationship with them if at all possible—or at least stay out of trouble with them. The most reliable indication of upper management's true priorities are those in which their pronouncements and activities appear to be consistent.

Cultural Differences

> The price of continued deviation from a group norm is
> rejection.
> —Robert J. Blake & Jane S. Mouton.

We are all subject to some form of cultural influence, as each of us was brought up *somewhere*. These influences sculpt our habits and our values, whether we realize it or not. Often, the first time we become consciously aware of our standards is when we come into close contact with people who have different ways of seeing things.

Wherever we may work we encounter cultural differences ranging from dress to ethics. Some establishments enforce rigid material standards: One New Jersey-based international delivery company prohibits employees from eating and drinking (even coffee) at their desks; others have relaxed their dress codes almost entirely. Legal and investment firms promote their own varieties of ethics; financial institutions tend toward conservativism, while journalism and education may be more liberally inclined.

If you work for or deal with a foreign firm, you are advised to heighten your sensitivities to their customs and ways of doing business. The rule of thumb that serves us well both here and abroad is to observe and listen. When in Rome (i.e., in Italy, Georgia, or New York) watch what the locals do, then seek a workable compromise between their behavior and what is comfortable for you. If you don't want to or are unable to conform to the local norm, consider leaving while it's still your choice.

The Tactics of Fitting In

> There is a written and an unwritten law.
> —Diogenes

Whatever the company culture, fitting in depends on recognizing and assuming the attitudes and behaviors that succeed in the environment, and avoiding the ones that don't.

Appearance

> Clothes make the man. Naked people have little or no influence in society.
> —Samuel Langhorne Clemens (alias Mark Twain)

A recent college graduate at a textbook publishing company was reprimanded by her boss for dressing too casually (in blue jeans). "Why should it matter what you wear," she asked, "if you do your work well?" We countered, "Why make an issue of something so trivial, when there are so many other areas where you can express your individuality in a more meaningful and acceptable manner?"

The point, of course, is that every organization has its own standards of dress, grooming, and adornment that contribute to an overall "look." People who depart from these parameters draw attention to their appearance and, often, disapproval. *Why* this is so is a lively topic for psychologists, sociologists, anthropologists, and historians; *that* it happens to be true is of greater relevance to your career. Rebels are advised to first establish their credentials and win the respect and admiration of their peers and employers before allowing their appearance to become an issue of focus.

Office Etiquette

> If you're going to play the game properly you'd better know every rule.
> —Barbara Jordan

One can only watch what people do and try to act accordingly. Does one address the CEO by his or her first name? Who is authorized to call a meeting? Do flex hours mean that you can show up any time you like, or are you expected to be at work during certain core hours? To what extent is it okay to use the phone for personal calls? Which managers can be disagreed with, and in what manner? By what criteria are people evaluated? Are you in step or waltzing to a merengue?

Hierarchy

> It is not sufficient that I succeed—all others must fail.
> —Genghis Khan

Know your place on the pyramid, and that of the people with whom you interact. The higher your position, the fewer and more dangerous your colleagues. The closer to the top, the more scrutiny and criticism you are subjected to from all sides. Make friends, create alliances, and choose your enemies quite carefully.

An establishment's culture is often made up of a "hidden network of personal relationships," according to strategic planner Meg Shinn of Oklahoma City. "If your ideas run counter to this culture, you can get yourself in trouble in a hurry. I used to work for a very political company where I was on the Steering Committee. How naive I was—I actually believed that committee meetings were a frank and open forum where you could say what was truly on your mind.

"My mistake was to disagree with someone who I thought was more or less on my own level who was saying something that was wrong. I couldn't understand why no one else took exception with his point, because it was such obvious nonsense I couldn't have been the only one to notice it. After the meeting, one of the people took me aside and straightened me out in a hurry. To make a long story short, the guy I was trying to contradict was a personal favorite of the CIO, and arguing with him was political suicide. By the time I found out why he was so special to the CIO," Meg added, "—and that's another story altogether—it was too late to patch things up with him."

The Honeymoon

> A bad beginning makes a bad ending.
> —Euripides

The first few weeks on a new job often set the tone. They can be the calm before the storm or the honeymoon leading to a solid relationship. Be aware that every organization plays the same game with slightly different rules. Focus on gaining familiarity with the environment, the people, and their goals and priorities in order to find out what is expected of you. As a new employee, it is important to show your willingness and ability to fit into the existing framework; as a manager or supervisor, it's a good idea to avoid making any significant changes until you have a better idea of why things are the way they are and whose toes you may be stepping on.

Establishing Credibility

> The dress of a wise man must be free of stains.
> —Moses Maimonides

Credibility must be established and maintained on every level of employment and responsibility. This is one of the pillars on which confidence and loyalty are based. It means that people can count on you to do the things you say you will. The process begins as soon as you join a new organization or department and continues as you rise up the hierarchy.

A leader's credibility sets the stage for everybody else. As a Kuwaiti army officer complained unhappily: "How can one cheerfully accept the fact that my superior officer, who fled the country on the very first day of the invasion, while I spent seven months in an Iraqi jail, is here again with a higher rank?" (*Le Monde*, Paris, May 11, 1995.)

Overcoming Obstacles

> Whatever women do they must do twice as well as men
> to be thought half as good. Luckily this is not difficult.
> —Charlotte Whitton (former mayor of Ottawa)

Prejudicial attitudes that favor certain groups or individuals over others are a lingering reality. If you are a member of a minority group, it may be prudent to check out the track records of your company, your department, and your boss. Seek out other members of your group within the organization and discreetly ask what they may have observed in this regard. Try to network with people to whom you may have a cultural affinity, or seek a sympathetic mentor; if you've been penalized because of your uniqueness, why not use it to advantage when you can? If there seems to be little opportunity for you, consider your options realistically: You can content yourself with whatever comes your way, fight to cut a path through the forest, or cut out for greener pastures. It takes a special person and a great deal of fortitude to fight against prevailing attitudes ...for every Jackie Robinson there are a million broken hearts.

Creating Opportunities

> When opportunity knocks, open the door.
> —Ruhtra

A culture can be a doorway to opportunity. Immigrants succeed or fail not only on their willingness to work hard, but also on their ability to recognize differences and opportunities in their new home. Often people who are immersed within the culture cannot see the forest for the trees.

> **Sometimes it works:** We heard about an entrepreneurial granny from Nairobi, Kenya, who opened a beer bar in the back of a do-it-yourself laundry with the sign, "Enjoy our suds while you wash your duds." Her daughter ran the bar, her grandson collected the quarters from the machines, and she made sure that there were always plenty of suds available for her happy customers.

Study your company's top performers and find out what influences their thinking. Orient yourself in productive directions. The opportunities are there; if the effort isn't worth your while, others will be glad to plant their feet beneath your desk.

The Competition

> To govern mankind one must not overrate them.
> —Lord Chesterton.

When two hikers saw a grizzly bear coming toward them, one quickly took off his boots and pulled on his sneakers. The other snickered at him. "Don't you realize that a grizzly can outrun a man?" "Of course," the first retorted, "I just want to be sure that I can outrun *you*."

To compete successfully in any culture you must clearly identify the competition. Most often this is not another company but your fellow workers and colleagues. B. F. Skinner suggested that cooperation could be set up more easily than competition, although that was when the world was a less crowded place. The best we can hope for today is a truce where people join together, temporarily, in order to compete with other groups. When their perception of their best interests shifts, cooperation disappears and individual competition, or new teams, emerge.

The Rules of the Game

> ..leadership knows right away who is with them and
> who is against them.
> —Pat Riley

Company objectives rely on people to fulfill them. Upper management selects their leaders initially from among those they trust and only secondarily from among those who may be qualified to do the job. Loyalty is their chief concern: They want team players who can be relied upon to play the game *their* way.

Office Politics

> 'Tis a hard winter when one wolf eats another.
> —*The Book of 1000 Proverbs*

Politics is networking (Chapter 16). Office politics ranges from being friendly with the receptionist to having allies among the career brokers and decision makers. It is vital to be politically aware of the people who can help and hurt you.

Teamwork

> All for one and one for all.
> —Alexandre Dumas (*The Three Musketeers*)

In today's complex world few of us can really go it alone. Cooperation is needed to harness the abilities of several people into a coordinated effort, and teamwork has evolved as the working culture of the 1990's. In the corporate environment, your best efforts can rebound in your face if you neglect to involve other people and gain their support.

> One step by 100 persons is better than 100 steps by one person.
> —Koichi Tsukamoto

Teamwork is based on the idea of coordinating the strengths of several individuals toward a common objective, as in war and sports. In theory, the potential rewards to be derived from matching skills and experience are greater than the sum of individual efforts. A significant side benefit is that the inexperienced members of the team gain from exposure to the more accomplished. From the company's perspective, this is an attractive concept.

Making the Best of Things

> He [Nicaraguan dictator Anastasio Somoza] may be a son of a bitch, but he's our son of a bitch.
> —attributed to Franklin D. Roosevelt

According to Moscow Communist Party chief and Politburo member Lev Zaikov, once the Politburo members reached an agreement, there were no objectors left. You played for the team or you were cut from the team, a rather unpleasant alternative.

Loyalty and teamwork are important issues to employers, so do your best to make them work for you. If you do not accept them, consider career alternatives that emphasize individual achievement.

CAREER BUSTER 12

IF YOU DON'T ADJUST TO CHANGE, YOUR SURVIVAL NICHE IS SHRINKING

..For the times they are a-changin'.
—Bob Dylan (Robert Zimmerman)

In this timeless line, a rock and roll poet captured the imagination and attention of an entire generation. It has since been quoted in a wide variety of contexts even by people who have never heard Bob Dylan sing: The subculture has exploded into acceptability. And now many of those who attended Dylan's concerts and bought his records are scratching their heads in bemusement over the preferences and ideas of their own children. The patterns of change are enticingly familiar, even in our reluctance to accept them.

Species, groups, and individuals keep pace with change or fade into history. When a culture fosters conditions of change, and then cannot meet the demands imposed by this change, it goes the way of the dinosaurs. There are similarities in the rise and decline of modern corporations. Some endure and prosper, while others struggle merely to survive. This is because the talents and policies that get you where you are don't necessarily take you any further; and also because influential leaders and decision makers are eventually replaced by new and different people who are more or less effective. In 1968, *Forbes* profiled the ten most profitable U.S. companies; by 1988, seven of the ten were out of favor: three no longer functioned independently, and four were barely making ends meet.

Change filters down from official decisions, hidden policies, and complex conditions, often as an unexpected side effect. New guidelines and requirements replace the old, and we need to adjust to and assimilate these differences. But we also have a natural tendency toward familiar habit patterns and comfort zones. We cling to what we know and shy away from the uncertain. We want to hold onto what we have acquired—our possessions and our status—and so we are inclined to influence or oppose certain change. Yet the inevitable cannot be long postponed, much less avoided. This conflict is our paradox: We recognize that change is unavoidable, and still we try our best to control, resist, or simply ignore it.

The times are always changing, although the more things change, the more we seem to wish they were the same.

CAREER SAVERS
The Nature of Change
The Art of Change
The Tactics of Change

The Nature of Change

> It is not that the future is slow in coming; it's that it is coming for only some of us.
> —Robert B. Reich.

Change is not a series of events that differ from one another, but an ebb and flow of all that was and is. Time, motion, and entropy are elements as well as agents of change. The world is altered as it spins. The nature of change is a continuum, a river of events in which our lives are swept along like grains of sand; the art of change is in the way we accept, adjust to, and use it. Our attitude toward change may be our greatest form of art.

The Art of Change

> God changes not what is in a people, until they change what is in themselves.
> —The Koran (13:11)

Change is a natural process to which most living things conform or die. Civilization devotes much of its energy toward controlling change: Nuclear fission, genetic engineering, and pollution are among our major achievements in this pursuit. Once released, however, many of our creations do not remain in our control.

"Without a fuller understanding of the wider nature of change," say Ian Morrison and Greg Schmid (Future Tense: The Business Realities of the Next Ten Years), "management fads come and go with a regularity that oftentimes exacerbates rather than resolves the fundamental longer-term problems."

The Tao Te Ching, written by Lao-tzu some six centuries ago, advises us to keep in step with the changing forces of nature. Indian Buddhism and Japanese Zen teach harmony and interdependence with nature. The ancient *I Ching* (Book of Change) emphasizes the balance between *consistency* and *change*—for the patterns of change are amazingly consistent. In the West, our Industrial Revolution was largely based upon a framework in which the effects of five fundamental sorts of change could interact: agriculture, population, technology, commerce, and transportation. Then the poets and economists took turns predicting changes certain to occur and trying to interpret those that already had.

> "The art of change is knowing how to solve new problems," securities analyst Marty Boyer of Pittsburgh says. "When the treadmill speeds up or slows down, you've got to change your pace accordingly. Every day the market changes, and so do your clients' situations. You have to make adjustments—a strategy that worked yesterday may fail today."

The More Things Change... The pace of change accelerates with each passing microchip. From messenger to fax, from telephone to modem—successful people keep up with the latest developments and take advantage of them. Openness to change is like knowing how to swim ..or at least to float until you have decided on a direction. The alternatives are to drown or to stay out of the water.

Technology has accelerated the pace of change. Available information and the speed with which it is delivered far exceed the agility of our brains, and so we have computers to collect, distill, and apply it for us. Fortunately, the details of change are new only at first. In time, the patterns grow increasingly familiar.

The More They Remain the Same

> Nothing endures but change.
> —Heraclitus

The seasons are our favorite metaphor for change: Summer differs from winter, and no two springtimes are exactly alike. And yet they blend together into patterns in which we find a comforting familiarity.

> Cal has been a supervisor with the Department of Education in Washington, D.C., for nearly 20 years. "Every few years," he says with a shrug, "they bring in a new chief and a few high-level appointees, you know, this senator's brother-in-law's son, that representative's second cousin, and they call a meeting to tell us how everything is going to be different. Democrats, Republicans, northerners, southerners, liberals, conservatives—for all their talk, hardly anything ever really changes

around here. They come and they go, and meanwhile I'm still here, me and the others like me. And you know," he continued philosophically, "they're lucky we're here, because we're the ones that keep this place running."

Chameleons have developed the ability to change color in response to light, heat, and other stimuli. It is a chameleon's nature to blend into its environment; by changing, it behaves like a true chameleon. Humans also learn to modify their images by the way they dress, speak, and behave. Allegiances are switched, points of view revised, and even recollections of fact may be altered in the name of *flexibility*. Those who "stick to their guns" occasionally triumph, though more often open minds prevail.

Few of the changes we perceive in business, education, politics, and the behavior of other people are inconsistent. In fact, most of these events and trends follow recognizable patterns if we take the time to think about them. Just as clever analysts may succeed in predicting changes in the stock market, staff reductions are often heralded by corporate consolidations, budget cuts, thinly veiled pronouncements, and rumor well in advance of the fact.

Harvey Hohauser, who operates an executive placement company out of Troy, Michigan, says that "Alert executives and managers are rarely caught by surprise, unless they become so ego-involved that they believe they're immune to bad news. There may be a few exceptions, like secret power plays and so on, but for the most part, your antenna is bound to pick up signals about major moves as long as you're paying attention."

Leaders have a vested interest in maintaining control of their domains. For this reason, major alterations of corporate philosophy and bureaucratic patterns are addressed with great reluctance. Growth ..reorganization ..downsizing ..these are buzzwords for the traditional techniques that many organizations use to avoid meaningful change. Some aspects of business remain fairly stable while others are in constant flux. Perhaps a better word than *flux* is *motion*, for most of the conditions that affect our careers pursue established routes. If life seems like a rollercoaster, remember that no matter how fast the rollercoaster cars may spin, they always follow their tracks. If you close your eyes the ride may make you dizzy, but if you study the rails and learn the turns, it will seem much smoother.

The Tactics of Change

..give us grace to accept with serenity the things that
cannot be changed, courage to change the things which
should be changed, and the wisdom to distinguish the
one from the other.
—Reinhold Niebuhr

The "average" worker in the U.S. changes jobs every four years,
whether by choice or necessity. Such statistics are misleading, however, for some job changes take place within the same company and
require less adjustment than moving to a different employer; and
some moves (e.g., in law, real estate, sales, and securities) involve
similar work with many of the same clients.

A more useful view of change is the rapid evolution of the marketplace and the need to respond effectively to new and different
conditions. Baseball is a microcosm of the pace of business in the
1990's: Batters must instantly adjust to the location and velocity of
the pitch, pitchers alter their approach between right-handers and
lefties, and team owners and coaches revise their plans to compensate for changing personnel from one season to the next. Those on
both sides of the checkbook who can quickly make the necessary adjustments usually succeed, while those who cannot do so fail.

Recognizing Change

It is a bad plan that admits of no modification.
—Publilius Syrus

The most practical way to keep pace with change is to recognize it,
react to it, and when appropriate, initiate it. Anticipating change enables you to prepare for and react to new conditions with purpose
and control, and possibly to initiate creative new directions. Passively waiting for things to happen can leave you victimized by change,
groping to survive, uncertain about your immediate future.

Timkin Co., whose headquarters are located in Canton, Ohio, is the
world's oldest, largest, and most profitable manufacturer of tapered
roller bearings. In 1994, Timkin spent more than half its profits
researching new materials and better methods and manufacturing
processes. Chief Executive Joseph F. Toot, Jr., claims that they have stayed
in first place by looking only ahead, never toward the past. "Today's
bearing is a dramatically different product than it was ten years ago, and I
would be very surprised if the 2005 version is anything like what we're
making now." (Forbes, March 13, 1995.)

The world changes ..today they serve Molotov cocktails
in restaurants.

The fourfold increase in destructive storms in recent years is creating
havoc among insurance companies (*Der Spiegel,* March 20, 1995,
Hamburg, Germany). Insurance executives "see themselves as the
first victims of the greenhouse effect, which is pushing the Earth's
wind machine to higher and higher speeds." Gerhard Berz, a meteo-
rologist at Münchener Rück—the world's largest reinsurance firm—
stated that they were increasingly certain that global warming is "influencing the frequency and severity of natural disasters."

A company's ability to survive and thrive in a changing business
environment is based on the ability of individuals—whether office or
factory workers—to adjust to the evolving needs of their employers.
Often top-level policies take weeks or even months to filter down to
the middle-management and staff levels; the manager who takes the
lead in introducing and implementing changes that are in accord
with brand new policies gains a reputation for being an alert and innovative leader.

> Past ideas that once worked determine approaches to
> new problems.
> —James Hillman

The best thing about change is that it forces you to consider different ways of solving problems, and to reconsider older methods. Personnel and economic changes are continually opening windows and
abruptly slamming them shut. A shift of management may offer an
opportunity to advance suggestions or to reposition yourself—new
department heads and project leaders may be open to your suggestions and offers of assistance. Opportunities exist almost everywhere, although individuals are often wise to seek them where they
are, and are likely to be, most plentiful. According to the U.S. Bureau
of Labor Statistics, the home care health services are expected to
more than double over the next decade, closely followed by systems
analysis and software engineering, physical therapy, desktop publishing, and the social services (especially occupational therapy and
counseling). Medical, legal, and technical support services and the
education, recreation, and security fields are also very promising. On
the other hand, many other occupations (like computer programming, printing, bank telling, farm work, and bartending) are drying
up. The trend in many areas is away from specialization and toward
adaptability and problem-solving skills.

Reacting to Change

> Don't fight forces; use them.
> —Richard Buckminster Fuller

The most serious challenge to adjusting to new conditions is force of habit. Resistance to change is a self-defeating pattern that can suffocate your career. Learning to react promptly and wisely to change is a more productive habit to cultivate. Success often depends on how well we adapt to change and how quickly we react to the opportunities it can offer.

If you don't adjust to the changes that affect your life and career, your survival niche grows ever smaller and eventually disappears. Adaptability means more than acquiring the skills needed for different kinds of work conditions (Chapter 6), but also adopting whole new sets of principles for building and maintaining your career. This may mean moving from technical to managerial areas, or vice versa, or becoming more entrepreneurial in the way you market and apply your trade.

> Citicorp Chairman John Reed had a reputation as a cold, driven, numbers-oriented personality as he rose through the ranks. But when he moved into the office of Chairman in 1984, he is said to have changed his former authoritarian ways and become more open and congenial. Reed's rationale was that he couldn't run the entire organization as a manager barking orders, but would have to adapt instead into the role of a leader setting a tone and direction.

Not all managers are as flexible to changing conditions as the British media executive who entered his office one afternoon to find his (male) assistant and (female) secretary in a heated embrace atop his desk. "Would you mind making some room?" he asked with classical English restraint, "I've got things to do." (Nicola Cole, Gemini News Service, London, May 30, 1995.)

Habits and beliefs are only changed through substitution. The stronger the pattern, the greater the need for a powerful alternative. Just as it is nearly impossible to kick the smoking habit without substituting a more desirable practice, you aren't likely to stop thinking negative thoughts (*I can't possibly accomplish this; why do I have such bad luck when it counts*) by simply telling yourself to stop. In both cases a substitute is needed, e.g., chewing gum or drinking tea for smoking, and a pattern of positive thoughts to counter pessimism (*I can make this work; my luck has changed*).

Your ability to change existing habits depends in large measure on your attitude and your assessment of the way things are. Are you content with your current circumstances? Are you willing to make the effort needed to change them? Do you believe in your ability to make these changes? By way of encouragement, consider that virtually every negative thought and behavior pattern that you have has been shared—and overcome—by someone else. It's possible because it has already been done, and if others can do it, so can you!

Reengineering

> Our ideas are only intellectual instruments which we use to break into phenomena; we must change them when they have served their purpose ...
> —Claude Bernard

If drastic change is needed in your life, you may wish to consider self-reengineering. This calls for a fresh assessment of the way you view yourself, your approach to the things you do, and your rationale for doing them.

In *Reengineering Yourself,* Daniel Araoz and William Sutton propose a "holistic approach" that integrates the experience you have gained throughout your lifetime. They offer a structured method designed to help you "to become your own creator, the CEO of your life." The utility of a thorough reevaluation of your perceptions, values, habits, and approaches depends on your personal circumstances and the degree of your dissatisfaction with your career. Are you seeking to integrate improvements into your work patterns or a more abrupt reversal of direction?

Initiating Change

> His (man's) imagination, his reason, his emotional subtlety and toughness, make it possible for him not to accept the environment but to change it.
> —Jacob Bronowski

Taking the initiative doesn't necessarily mean that you must grab the bull by its horns. In fact, there are more propitious ways to become an innovator. To some, initiating changes that are in harmony with the environment in which they work is second nature, while others have to be coaxed as if by matadors.

▼▼▼

If you've got them by the balls, their hearts and minds
will soon follow.
—Charles Colson (Special Assistant to President Nixon)

The most effective way to encourage people to adopt new ways of
doing things is to explain to them the nature, purpose, and advantages of the change, their role in it, and the consequences if the pre-
scribed change does not occur. W. R. Grace CEO Peter Grace was
quoted in *Financial World* (April 5, 1988) as saying that "You must
keep people scared every day." However, a heavy hand more often
discourages initiative and efficiency in the long run. We prefer positive encouragement, support, and consistency.

Author Alvin Toffler defines *future shock* as "the shattering
stress and disorientation that we induce in individuals by subjecting
them to too much change in too short a time." Abrupt and imposed
changes tend to meet with the most resistance, clouding the decision
process with emotion. Like the stubborn captain, who saw what ap-
peared to be the lights of another ship moving toward his vessel:

"Tell them to change their course by fifteen degrees south," he
instructed his signalman.

"Change *your* course fifteen degrees south," came the reply.

The captain had another message sent: "This is Captain Blowhard. I
say again, change your course fifteen degrees south."

"This is seaman first class Lowly. I repeat, change *your* course to
the south."

As the captain's ship grew ever closer to the light, he urgently
insisted: "This is a battleship. For the last time, change your course to
the south."

The final word, however, came from the young seaman. "This is a
lighthouse. Change *your* course south."

Resisting Change

It is the nature of a man as he grows older to protest
against change, particularly change for the better.
—John Steinbeck

One of the most self-defeating concepts ever invented is contained in
the saying, "better the Devil we know." Such negative reasoning encourages us to hold onto mistaken, unprofitable, and even damaging
views and habits because of fear of the unknown. We call it spiritual paralysis: the art of justifying mediocrity and failure.

▼▼▼

Change continues to dictate necessity. Over time, our careers and lives are likely to depend on our ability to deal with changing realities and requirements. Once you have recognized the need for change, why not view it as a challenge? Create an inner dialogue to talk yourself into a positive frame of mind. If you know you've got to do something, an upbeat attitude is guaranteed to work in your behalf.

A frog can sit in a pool of water without noticing a gradual rise or drop in temperature. Executives, managers, and workers who are similarly insensitive to change risk having their careers completely cooked or frozen solid. A case in point, Great Britain, and in particular, Triumph, were once the world leaders in producing and selling motorcycles. Their reluctance to modernize product development and production enabled Japanese manufacturers to decimate the British market share from 80% to less than 1%.

Some cultures are incapable of making the adjustments needed to survive: In 1973, Captain Jacques-Yves Cousteau's research team studied Chile's 37 remaining Qawashqar Indians. By 1988 there were none left—they were incapable of adjusting to the mines where they were sent to work and passed into extinction.

CAREER BUSTER 13

HOW CAN YOU SUCCEED AT A JOB THAT TURNS YOU OFF?

> ..the first hundred years are the hardest.
> —Wilson Mizner

One of the most difficult questions is when to stay the course and when to move on down the road. Sometimes the decision is easy—for example, when it is made for us, or when considerably better opportunities are available. More often we find ourselves attempting to evaluate nuances and weigh uncertain pluses against potential minuses.

Whether to remain with your current position or company or to make a move is too important a decision to be left to mood or happenstance. Many people enjoy rewarding careers with one or two employers, while others find success by moving around more frequently. There is no formula to follow, but there are guidelines that can help us match our individual circumstances to the external realities in which we find ourselves. This chapter talks about mobility and security in today's job market, and how to recognize and cope with signs of burnout.

CAREER SAVERS

The Art of Mobility
The Tactics of Job Security
Coping with Burnout

The Art of Mobility

> And what's a life?—a weary pilgrimage ...
> —Francis Quarles

Mobility is as much a frame of mind as picking yourself up and going somewhere else. *Knowing* that you have options is even more important than exercising them, for it is in the knowledge that we find confidence and a sense of security. Professional mobility means having the ability to move, owning the option of leaving your current position for another (preferably better, but certainly no worse) job. You don't have to move in order to be mobile, you just need an open ticket to ride.

> We are surrounded by insurmountable opportunities.
> —Pogo

Opportunities come and go; some are worth taking, others not. New openings may seem appealing until we analyze them closely, especially their similarities to and differences from our current situations. Is the difference in responsibilities, salary, working conditions, people, or commuting time significant? What are the potential advantages and disadvantages? Are the things you don't like about your current place likely to change by accepting the new job? What do you stand to gain and lose by staying and by leaving?

There are valid reasons for remaining where you are and also for moving on. Change (Chapter 12) for the sake of change is misguided and potentially damaging when indulged in too often, although there are definitely times when a change of scenery is called for. The art of mobility is knowing when to hold 'em and when to fold 'em.

Issues

> Man's happiness in life is the result of man's own effort ...
> —Ch'en Tu-hsiu

Boredom, politics, a lack of opportunity, or discovering that you're in the wrong job are signs that change is needed. If you can improve conditions for yourself, by all means do so; otherwise, you need to begin looking around to see what's out there.

> Monotonously the lorries sway, monotonously come the calls, monotonously falls the rain.
> —Erich Maria Remarque

When Leonardo da Vinci said that "Iron rusts from disuse; stagnant water loses its purity and in cold weather becomes frozen .." he was really talking about people. People, who fall into ruts and routines into which days and months and even years can disappear within a fog of memory that leaves us little joy or comfort for our efforts.

Each of us is bored some of the time, for many of the patterns that sustain our lives are too familiar to excite attention. Much of habit is a comfort, but in excess it hypnotizes, paralyzes, numbs the senses into submission. Over time, routine leaches more energy than effort and to less avail. If your daily routine is dull and uninspiring, devoid of challenge, joy, or even anger, you may be on the road to burnout.

> Politicians are the same all over. They promise to build
> bridges, even where there are no rivers.
> —Nikita Khrushchev

Have you been getting passed over for promotions and interesting assignments by people no more skilled and experienced than you? Do you attribute this to office politics? If you don't fit into the corporate culture (Chapter 11), it will be tough if not impossible for you to advance and you have a decision to make: Learn to play with the *in crowd*, or look for an environment to which you're better suited.

> Everything has an end.
> —Masai Proverb

The following story comes from a friend who recently retired from the New York City garment industry after a career of over 50 years.

"In 1945, a firm was established for the conversion of a new fabric called nylon. Since it was new, nylon did not fall under the control of the OPS (Office of Price Stabilization), and so there was no limit to the price that could be charged for it. With the help of an expanding economy and a war, the firm quickly grew from five to over a hundred employees and $40 million in sales within ten years.

In 1955, the president decided to buy out his partner (who had the original contract with Dupont), thus becoming sole owner. He then promised certain key employees that he would issue stock in the company in order to give them shares, but his promise was not kept. Instead he handed out bonuses like mink coats and even a car, but never shares of stock or money. Those who knew him speculated that the owner didn't want his employees to accumulate enough cash to go into business for themselves (as he had done).

By 1959, it was apparent that the owner planned to keep the business intact for a son who was now in college. Staff members finally realized that their careers had come to a dead end. After having devoted so many years to the company, embittered employees, managers, and department heads began leaving. When the owner died, his son (a Wharton graduate) took over the business. But without a cadre of experienced managers and staff, the firm went bankrupt within three years."

Staying

> The best way to change a situation is to imagine that you
> will stay right where you are the rest of your life.
> —Gary Snyder

John Lax, a retired educational publishing professional living in St. Charles, Illinois, warns about the risks of family-owned businesses, where nepotism may restrict opportunities. He recounts the story of a well-known publishing company that used to require their mid-management level staff to undergo interviews with a consulting firm.

"One employee, who headed a prestigious and profitable program, began to sense that he wasn't doing well during his interview. In an attempt to turn things around, he asked if there was a human profile from which the questions were derived. The proud response was 'Yes, it is your president, John Marriedwell!'

"The interviewee—call him Sigmund in honor of his perception—responded, 'If you had told me this at the start I could have saved us both an hour.'

"'What do you mean?' asked the consultant.

"'I'm married,' said the employee.

"'What's that got to do with it?' asked the consultant.

"'I can't marry the (founder and) Chairman's daughter,' was the departing reply.

"The interviews were discontinued. Some time later (following a divorce proceeding), Mr. Marriedwell was terminated .. perhaps coincidently confirming Sigmund's thesis."

A Good Profession

> Everyone wants to be Cary Grant. Even I want to be
> Cary Grant.
> —Archibald Alexander Leach (Cary Grant)

A good profession, among other things, is one that's in demand. If the need for people in your line of work is strong, you're more likely to survive staff reductions, consolidations, and other budget-squeezing actions than people for whom the available supply of qualified talent exceeds the need. If the demand is shrinking, it may be prudent to consider career alternatives.

Numerous publications provide up-to-date information on job rankings. For example, a recent survey by the *New York Post* showed that the position of computer systems analyst had moved from 31st place in 1992 up to first in 1994. Physicians had inched up from 3 to

2, while psychologists jumped from 29 to 7, paralegals from 38 to 11, registered nurses from 52 to 28, and construction superintendents all the way from 66 to 20. On the down side, biologists fell from first to 16th place, mathematicians from 4 to 27, veterinarians from 10 to 35, lawyers from 18 to 43, and architects from 20 to 46.

Such surveys also list salary ranges, short- and medium-term outlooks, security ratings, prestige, and parts of the country where job opportunities are concentrated. For example, hotel managers (down from 40 to 72) earn an annual (median) salary of $54,000, with a 40% projected growth rate and best prospects in Las Vegas, Orlando, and Honolulu. Forest rangers (up from 59 to 36), who earn around $30,000, can look forward to only 12% growth and would have to do most of their prospecting in the Portland, Seattle, and Sacramento areas.

This type of information can help you to decide what to study in college, which additional courses to take, where and when to move (or stay put), and how aggressive you can afford to be in risking your current job.

> What is the secret of the trick? How did I get so old so quick?
> —Ogden Nash

Allen E. Murray, who served as Mobil Corporation's chairman of the board and CEO from 1986 to 1993 (and in many different roles since then), first joined Mobil in 1952 as an accountant.

Many companies continue to reward loyalty by promoting from within. The most meaningful way to verify a company's policy in this regard is to listen with half an ear to what they say and to observe with both eyes what they actually do. Is there a history of upward movement or of early retirements? Have a lot of people been stuck in the same jobs for years? When new employees are brought in, is it usually at the lower, middle, or upper end? Although this is important throughout the company, it is of particular significance in your division, department, or group. Finally, how have **you** been treated since you've been there? Be realistic in assessing your prospects. If you're in the wrong job or at a dead end, begin to explore alternatives.

Seeking Alternatives

> We must learn to explore all the options and possibilities that confront us in a complex and rapidly changing world.
> —James William Fullbright

If you move to another company, it's preferable to make the move on your own terms, that is, before losing your current job. So keep your feelers out via networking (Chapter 16), especially when you see or sense signs of trouble.

Making the Move

> When you come to a fork in the road, take it.
> —Yogi Berra

The National Study of the Changing Workforce conducted a survey to identify people's main reasons for accepting new positions. Fifty-nine percent of the respondents identified the nature of the work as their major consideration; 55% did it to gain new skills; and 35% for financial reasons. We didn't scrutinize the report to find out how these numbers could be made to fit into 100%, and we are always a bit skeptical about the validity of these types of surveys, e.g., whether people who are primarily motivated by financial concerns will admit this. Nevertheless, it is clear that people are increasingly concerned with the quality and directions of their careers.

There is no hard and fast rule about changing jobs or companies because not all employees follow the same rules. Some people spend their entire careers with the same employer, while others change frequently. One philosophy has it that staying in a single company for 20 years is a sign of rigor mortis; another holds that frequent change is a sign of instability. Generally, the time to move is when you *feel* it's right.

> Good night, good night! parting is such sweet sorrow,
> That I shall say good night till it be morrow.
> —William Shakespeare (*Romeo and Juliet*)

When you make up your mind to leave, keep it to yourself at work. Stay on good terms with everyone, just as if you were planning to remain where you are. Use your decision to energize yourself and, if possible, to raise the level of your current performance. An upbeat attitude will put you in a better frame of mind to interview and make things more bearable while you look for a new job.

Be careful not to burn any bridges behind you—you never know when you may have to ask for a favor or a recommendation. Before leaving, tie up any loose ends so as to minimize the criticism and blame after you're gone. This has the advantage of allowing you to maintain a positive relationship with your former employer, and it sets the tone for entering the new place with momentum and positive energy.

There was so much handwriting on the wall
That even the wall fell down.
—Christopher Morley

If your company, department, profession, or position appears vulnerable, consider these three points:

1. Are you in immediate danger of losing your job?
2. What is likely to happen over the next 3, 6, and 12 months if you stay where you are?
3. What will probably happen if you quit?

If your job is in serious jeopardy, can you take steps to save it? Are you prepared to make the effort? What is the probable time frame (using the least optimistic estimate)? If you're likely to lose your job, you may have no choice but to seek a new one. If the reason is personal, do what you can to correct any faults or negative impressions before leaving, or the same thing may happen again. Otherwise, chalk it up to experience and get ready to move on with confidence and enthusiasm.

If your current employment appears secure but you are unhappy in it, seek to enhance your job by adding responsibilities. If the problem is a lack of challenge or personality conflict, explore opportunities in other departments as well as outside the company. Use this time to reevaluate your career goals. Are you in the right profession, or is it time to consider a change?

> Fred M. was a commercial airline pilot. When his eyesight became a problem, he was offered a managerial position, which he turned down. Instead, he bought a farm. "I knew I couldn't hack a desk job," he said, "so I opted for a boyhood dream."

..it's time for a change.
—Thomas Dewey

There is conflicting evidence on whether employees keep their jobs as long as in the past or switch more often. The U.S. Labor Department, the U.S. Census Bureau, and the Employment Benefit Institute are among the sources that assure us of a general stability in the workforce, while many other observers insist that the contrary is true.

Sylvester J. Schieber of the Wyatt Company believes that people in today's workforce "look a lot like their folks." [Albert B.

Crenshaw, *Washington Post*]. In a *Wall Street Journal* interview, Betsy Collard of the Palo Alto, California, Career Action Center disagreed: "I find these studies hard to believe," she contended. "It doesn't jibe with most people's sense of the situation."

> "..it is often a comfort to shift one's position and be bruised in a new place."
> —Washington Irving

If you want to switch industries, your challenge is to convince decision makers that your skills and background are indeed transferable, and that hiring you is worth the risk to them. Do they have a track record of hiring from other industries? Have you made a similar switch before? Produce examples of others who have done so.

In 1986, Georgia Ryder was a municipal bond investment manager. She took off nine years to raise a family, and then rejoined her former company as a marketing consultant. Only half a year later, Georgia was appointed vice president of strategic marketing in a visible new area. How did this all happen?

"While I was busy having (two) babies, I served as president of my college alma mater board and managed a six-figure budget. I coordinated contributions to our college fund, organized fund-raisers and get-togethers, and directed marketing campaigns. I also maintained contact with a few people where I used to work. When I was ready to resume my career, I applied to my old employer as if I was entering the job market for the first time. I used a functional résumé that emphasized my new skills, not just employment experience. My strategy," she told us, "was to present myself as someone I'd be interested in if I were doing the hiring. And," she smiled, "it worked."

The Tactics of Job Security

> ..job security is a thing of the past.
> —Robert Barner

More than ever before, job security is tied to having marketable skills. The most loyal of employers can hit tough times or be bought out by groups with different management styles. Conversely, the faceless number-crunchers who could care less about your devoted years of service will pay to keep you if they feel they need you. Even civil service and other union-protected positions are subject to periodic renegotiation. The bottom line is that you need to secure your own career by positioning it wisely against the ebb and flow of the job market. You are more likely to *be* and *feel* secure by relying on your marketability rather than on other people's promises.

Stability vs Instability

> There is no security on this earth. There is only opportunity.
> —General Douglas MacArthur

The stability or instability of today's job market depends upon your interpretation of the signs. Where the experts disagree, we need to find our own way. According to Sylvester J. Schieber, the Wyatt Company (benefits consulting, Washington, D.C.), "The typical worker today does not change companies more frequently than someone the same age 20 years ago, contrary to popular perceptions."

Yet Peter Weddle, Chairman and CEO of Job Bank USA, points out that close to 4.3 million jobs have been eliminated by the Fortune 500 companies since 1980. That's nearly 1,000 fewer jobs a day, and it doesn't count the thousands of other employers.

However, an article by Gabrielle Solomon (*National Business Employment Weekly,* April 16-22, 1995) reassures us that ..."a good percentage of employees are enjoying old-fashioned job security." Ms. Solomon refers to a *Wall Street Journal* article citing the views of Princeton University's Henry Farber, a professor of industrial relations. "It just isn't true that long-term employment is a thing of the past," Professor Farber is quoted as saying. "I don't see anything in the data to suggest a massive change in career patterns."

Others find Farber's numbers hard to fathom, for a sense of change and instability appears prevalent from coast to coast. One factor not reflected by the statistics is that jobs and responsibilities within a company are increasingly subject to change. When Hewlett-Packard boasts that 55% of their employees have been with them for over ten years, we can probably assume a good deal of mobility within the corporation.

What does all this mean? That you've got to assess your own industry, your employer, and your (perceived) value to whoever signs your checks in order to determine the degree of your job security.

Marketable Skills

> ..how little security we have when we trust our happiness in the hands of others.
> —William Hazlitt

Marketable skills are the only meaningful form of job security. If they need piano players, they aren't hiring even the most brilliant engineers or veterinarians; and if the market is glutted with candidates in whatever field you're studying, consider changing your major even if it means staying in college another year or two.

In technical environments, expertise is valued only as long as the topic is in vogue. The ability to stay abreast of change may serve you better than becoming the world's leading expert in a dying field. Here as elsewhere, management skills are valued, especially if you're skilled at getting people to produce.

> My job is so secret that even I don't know what I'm doing.
> —(CIA director) William Webster

Dale Carnegie believed that specialization was one of the keys to success, as anyone who has a highly valued (and well-paid) niche might be inclined to agree. Of course, this formula only works while the specialty is needed. The problem with specializing is the limits it imposes on your career—you may find it harder to change the nature of your work once it is out of vogue or has become tedious.

In large organizations, generalists risk losing their jobs during belt-tightenings and restructures unless they represent a recognized value. However, few small- to mid-sized companies can afford the luxury of specialists and so are inclined toward workers who can wear several hats at once.

> In order to be irreplaceable one must always be different.
> —Coco Chanel

> "How have you managed to survive four new administrations?" a bureaucrat was asked by his new supervisor. "They can't get rid of me," the fellow answered, "I'm much too far behind in my work."

No one is irreplaceable, although there are people who make a living by convincing others that they are. The closest most of us can come to irreplaceability is to develop special skills and knowledge that would cost our employers a lot of time, money, and inconvenience to replace. Then we only need to avoid annoying them too much.

> How'm I doing?
> —(former New York City mayor) Ed Koch

Self-evaluation is partially based on your perception of how others rate you and your own personal sense of the way that things are going. Measure your progress by comparing past accomplishments to recent ones. Set yourself periodic goals that can be achieved within a specified period, and then celebrate (if only to yourself) your achievements. This will help you to evaluate your performance and your level of satisfaction in your current position.

> If at first you don't succeed, destroy all evidence that you tried.
> —Newt Hielscher

Reengineering is one of the buzzwords of our time. Generally, it means to re-do a system or a process to make it more efficient. Human reengineering is the process of taking a long, hard look at your career and life, deciding to make some (major or minor) changes, and then making them. It means reevaluating your situation, and perhaps your values and objectives, and getting yourself ready to do whatever must be done to get you where you want to be. Daniel Araoz and William Sutton (*Reengineering Yourself*) make the point that whatever got you where you are now won't necessarily bring you to the next level; you need to learn what *will* get you there and then prepare for the next stage. And this may mean letting go of familiar patterns and ideas in order to focus on new skills and challenges.

> Simon Ling was a gifted computer software analyst. Success at designing systems led to promotions and, eventually, a middle-management position. Simon began to realize that his technical skills wouldn't help him as a manager, and so he sought to apply his analytical mind to a new discipline. He took a few psychology and management classes, observed other managers carefully, and found a mentor who knew little about computers but was a highly respected manager. "I had to develop an entirely new mind-set," he admitted to us. "Before, I paid hardly any attention to anyone who wasn't technical. But now I understand that it's the managers who make the important financial and other decisions that determine what the technical people spend their time on. Once I get into upper management, I can really influence the systems we develop, and I can also make sure that they're done the right way."

Coping with Burnout

> I came to serve you at the age of 28 and now I have not a hair on me that is not white, and my body is infirm and exhausted.
> —Christopher Columbus

Burnout is when fatigue replaces enthusiasm. It's when we aren't motivated to work any more. It dulls our sensitivity to change, growing almost imperceptibly out of frustration and anxiety, maturing into dissatisfaction and depression. When these feelings become pervasive, some of us are encouraged to give up. Fatigue that lasts beyond a good night's sleep or two may be burnout. It can result from pressure at work or home—the continued effort to achieve in the face of mounting competition.

Rising levels of job dissatisfaction in certain professions appear largely related to stress resulting from longer hours on the job, less time at home, pressure to make partner, and lower esteem in the community. Of course, the goals and requirements of your employer are only yours if you accept them. Is the threat of losing your job more terrible than coping with unnatural pressure? Are you putting so much pressure on yourself that you can't possibly satisfy your employer's standards and expectations, much less your own?

> Darryl K., a financial analyst, was suffering from the initial stages of burnout. "I was so worried about getting fired, I put more and more pressure on myself, until my wife sat me down and told me that it wasn't worth it. 'No damned job is worth this kind of aggravation,' she insisted, and we began to talk about it during evenings and weekends. I decided that my family life was more important. After all, there were other companies out there for people with my job skills. So I started taking things less—how can I explain this—not less seriously, but less personally, and you know what? I began to enjoy my work a lot more, and I even became a more effective analyst."

Ambrose Bierce defined achievement as "the death of endeavor and the birth of disgust." Presumably, he was referring to achievement as an end in itself rather than a single milestone along a lifelong path. Ohio State University psychologist Robert Arkin (*Chicago Tribune,* Sunday, August 20, 1995) describes overachievers as having "...a high burnout rate and [are] prone to nervous breakdowns, hospitalizations and collapsing, perhaps even in the workplace settings." Whereas *high* achievers tend to enjoy what they are doing.

The Peter Principle

> People tend to be promoted until they reach their level of incompetence.
> —Laurence J. Peter

John Quincy Adams, an unpopular president, was later elected to the House of Representatives, which proved (in the view of many) to be his highest level of competence. Unfortunately, few of us are afforded the opportunity to return to where we were last effective after having topped out a tad too high. For stepping back appears to be synonymous with failure. So we must cope with those around us who are firmly entrenched within their places of in-competence, as they must cope with those of us who've "Petered out."

Review your own status from time to time, especially after major job changes and promotions. Are you enjoying your new responsibilities? Are you getting similar satisfaction and feedback to that of your last position, or are you having a tough time adjusting? Do you feel that you are growing into your new responsibilities, or are you just growing frustrated?

Competition

> The trouble with the rat race is that even if you win, you're still a rat.
> —Lily Tomlin

The spirit of competition that inspires our best efforts incites as well the purest and most virulent form of antisocial behavior imaginable: One of us wins, and everybody else loses. In order to compete successfully in a competitive environment, we seek advantages through secrecy, artifice, and other uncooperative actions. We work to position ourselves to win—the ultimate goal—whatever the endeavor.

When one of our competitors gains the victory (over us), the best that we can do is use our sense of loss (failure, humiliation, disappointment) to spur our efforts on to greater intensity. When we win, there is little time to enjoy the victory because there is no guarantee that we will be successful the next time around.

Every normal person who is aware of potentially damaging consequences feels some distress. It's perfectly normal and healthy to be concerned about things that may hurt you. The difference lies in what you do about your anxieties: allow them to choke and immobilize you, or use them to motivate a thorough and energetic effort.

Motivation

> Motivation will almost always beat mere talent.
> —Norman Augustine

The antidote to burnout is motivation. That's what helps you to get started and to keep going when things are difficult. People who lack motivation are advised to set small, reachable goals, and to use them as a springboard to larger goals. Even small accomplishments can generate new energy and feelings of satisfaction.

Trying new or unfamiliar things can be scary, especially if you haven't yet established a track record of success. Reassurance and support can help you to get started and encourage you to take a chance. Once you have begun, it is important to acknowledge to yourself that you had the courage to make the attempt, no matter how it turned out. If your effort was successful, acknowledge that and use it to encourage you to move forward. Even if it turned out badly, give yourself credit for trying something new and use what you have learned to propel yourself forward.

> No one can make you feel inferior without your consent.
> —Eleanor Roosevelt

Self-confidence is the belief that you can do something. Real confidence is based upon experience and a positive self-image: I've done this (or something like it) before, so I can do it again; most of the things I've tried came out well enough, and when they didn't, I was able to deal with the consequences and improve upon the result. After all, other people are able to do this, so why not me?

Career Fitness

> No gain without pain.
> —Benjamin Franklin

The fitness of your career relies on your occupational strengths and your ability to protect yourself from hidden and career-threatening illnesses. Robert Barner (*National Business Employment Weekly,* April 22, 1995) advises potential burnout victims to "Start by breaking with the past and refocusing on the future." Looking forward and letting go of the past helps people to acknowledge the many opportunities available to them. Barner advises us to:

—Avoid obsolescence by keeping our skills current (especially computer literacy);

—Develop additional resources by networking and attending conferences; and

—Regroup periodically by reevaluating our goals and priorities.

Recognize that you are responsible for your own career, and that you can't afford to delegate that responsibility to other decision makers and corporations.

> Decay is inherent in all compounded things. Strive on with diligence.
> —Buddha

People who have dull and repetitive jobs may consider career alternatives. Some, with years of vested service, seek relief via outside interests. They use sports, social clubs, travel, hobbies, and personal relationships to enliven their routines and enhance their self-esteem. Taking classes and specialized training courses can renew your interest in your career while opening new doors and opportunities. "I sign up for an evening class in a local college almost every year," Edith Barry of Pensacola told us. "It renews my energy and interests, and it's fun to hang out with students many of whom are my own children's ages."

> A few years ago, Debra Dawson was the account supervisor of the Unisys account at the advertising giant, Young & Rubicam (*Forbes*, April 10, 1995). Aged 39, Debra was already caught up in an attack of midcareer burnout. "I thought I'd be better off doing something else," she decided. So she left Madison Avenue in favor of New England, and started up a successful software publishing company that expanded into the specialized medical arena.

CAREER BUSTER 14

BAD TIMING IS A WASTE OF EFFORT AND OPPORTUNITY

Men flourish only for a moment.
—Homer

To dancers, timing is primarily the synchronization of movement; to most of us, it means choosing the most opportune moment or period to act in order to achieve the best possible result. Since timing is somewhat intuitive, we call it an *art* in our book, whereas we refer to the *tactics* of time management.

Time management is intricately linked to the establishment of priorities (Chapter 9): Priorities are the reasons for choosing a particular path, while time management (and timing) determine when we take the path, the speed at which we travel, and when we stop to rest. Goals are based on principles and values; the management of time is a more mechanical process that follows carefully planned tactics. Most people recognize the importance of using time effectively. The problem with offering advice in this area is that timing and time management are woven into our individual styles, temperaments, needs, and capabilities. On the one hand, there are common-sense guidelines that apply across the board; on the other, not everything that works for one person can be transferred to someone else.

The principles, examples, and ideas presented in this chapter are intended to offer you an understanding of the realities and problems involved with timing and time management, and a practical array of solutions from which to pick and choose. We believe you'll find some of our suggestions worth your time.

CAREER SAVERS

The Art of Timing
The Sands of Time
The Tactics of Time Management

The Art of Timing

> It is circumstances and proper timing that give an action
> its character and make it either good or bad.
> —Agesilaus

Timing is both art and science. The former is a kind of common sense, while the latter requires thought and planning. Athletes and musicians rely heavily on timing, as do people who drive cars, navigate crowds on foot, or simply get out of bed in the morning. In other words, timing is essential to all of us in nearly everything we do.

Bad Timing

> We slip our opportunities; and if they be not catched in
> the very nick, they are irrevocably lost.
> —Seneca

Bad timing—the cause of most missed opportunities—is being out of synch. It's like trying to swim against the current, or not being ready to go with the current when it's flowing in the right direction. Bad timing is when you try to force an issue or are unprepared to recognize more favorable conditions.

> I've been on a calendar, but never on time.
> —Marilyn Monroe

Winston Churchill considered unpunctuality to be "a vile habit." To most successful people, arriving late for meetings and other obligations is rude and unacceptable. Accidents happen, but habitual lateness is unprofessional and insulting to the people you keep waiting. Sometimes being late can cost you dearly.

> In the movie *Disclosure,* the victim is set up by his scheming boss to
> arrive an hour after an important meeting has begun. His untimely
> appearance is remarked on with sarcasm by the top executive, resulting
> in a loss of face and credibility.

Your agenda isn't necessarily shared by others. Neither is your sense of urgency. When you want someone else to act or decide in your favor, you need to gain a sense of *their* agenda and priorities. Then try to present your objective in a manner that is in harmony with (or at least not contrary to) theirs.

> Julian asked for a raise at the worst possible time—while his boss was
> working on his annual status report, which was behind schedule (as

usual); he was annoyed at his staff (including Julian) because of the department's mediocre performance; and he had a headache. Unsurprisingly, he turned Julian down abruptly. Hannah, a colleague of Julian's, saw what happened to him and decided to wait for a more opportune occasion to ask for the promotion she rightly deserved. Unfortunately, the boss seemed always to be in a bad mood; the time was never quite right, and so she never got around to asking.

Good Timing

> ..right timing is in all things the most important factor.
> —Hesiod

Good timing is being at the right place at the right time and then being able to take advantage of the situation. If you are able to recognize and seize opportunities, your career will profit accordingly. But if you are unprepared when fortune smiles your way, you might as well stay home in bed.

> If you're there before it's over, you're on time.
> —James L. "Jimmy" Walker

Natasha knew that her department head, Mr. Higgins, often arrived early for weekly meetings, so she made a point of getting to the conference room even earlier. Whenever Higgins would show up, Natasha was already there writing in her notebook or reviewing a report. They began to chat together during the 5- to 10-minute periods before the other people arrived and got to know one another fairly well. Higgins began to ask for her opinion on various company issues, and eventually assigned Natasha an important project which led to a promotion. In this case, a quarter of an hour early was right on time.

> The best time to invest your money was 20 years ago; the next best time is now.
> —Chinese Proverb

The right time is when an opportunity presents itself, or when you have created one. Many people find it useful to attack whatever they want to do least and get it over with. Once the most unpleasant task is done, the rest of your day is likely to be smoother sailing. Or if the methodical approach suits you better, just arrange your tasks and go through them in whatever sequence you've decided.

Greg (who worked in the same department as Julian and Hannah) waited for what he felt to be the right moment—the completion of a project in which he had played a major role and which had been well-

received by management. He stated his case for a promotion clearly and
succinctly to his busy boss, who saw no reason to deny it. The boss
certainly wasn't going to give the promotion to Julian, whom he found
somehow annoying, or to Hannah who (as far as he knew) probably
didn't want it.

Off-Timing

> I took the (road) less travelled by,
> And that has made all the difference.
> —Robert Frost

Contrarians are those who take opposing views from the majority. In
the stock market, they buy when others sell and vice versa. Off-
timers travel pretty much the same roads as everybody else, but
when the crowds are thinner.

> In our nation's capital, there is a popular path near the Washington
> Memorial that is frequented by many famous and lesser-known figures.
> By 5 most mornings, any number of walkers and joggers have begun their
> day out there. It is said that the best time to get through to certain
> senators, representatives, and influential aides is to pull on your running
> shoes and jog alongside.

Waiting

> To know how to wait is the great secret of success.
> —Joseph Marie de Maistre

When you're kept waiting the shoe is on the other foot. While it is
rude and inconsiderate for someone else to keep you waiting, it does
happen, and you will have to deal with it from time to time. If you
get upset every time someone delays you, you'll burn yourself out
and very likely embarrass yourself as well. By being prepared to wait
with reading materials, a notebook, or perhaps a laptop computer,
you can preserve both the reality and the appearance of efficiency
and resourcefulness.

Procrastination is delay that results from inability to initiate an
action. If you are a procrastinator, you need to discipline yourself
into creating deadlines and schedules. Then force yourself to take a
small first step. Think about the consequences of not acting and use
that to motivate yourself. The point is to get started—once you do,
momentum tends to make each successive step much easier than the
last.

Taking advantage of *dead time* (e.g., travel time or time waiting in the doctor's office) can help you to prepare for, or take your mind off, an uncertain or unpleasant situation.

P.R., an IRS tax inspector, looks at blocks of 10 to 15 minutes or longer as ".. an opportunity to catch up on my reading."

Coping

> Think first, then act.
> —Pythagoras

There is always a fine line between being purposeful (focusing on your tasks) and rude, and it's up to you to draw that line. Emergencies and crises demand sharper focus, but "normal" times are when most crises are created or averted. Know when to delegate work and responsibilities—even if your subordinates can't do most jobs as well as you, some of them can probably do them well enough.

Jill is an airline executive who delegates all but about 5% of her tasks to her staff and spends the bulk of her time actively supplying them with guidelines, feedback, and directions. "This way I can keep in touch with most of my projects without getting bogged down in any of them," she told us, "and I can focus my attention on the special situations that require it."

Learn to minimize the impact of interruptions on your time and productivity without shutting yourself off and alienating fellow workers. Handling interruptions effectively and gracefully is a form of artful management.

Kate White, *Redbook* editor-in-chief, advises setting a time limit on unannounced visits. Example: "..come in. I have a few minutes before my next meeting." And Stephanie Winston, president of The Organizing Principle (a New York time management consulting company), counsels setting aside priority-task times during which we cannot be reached. (*Bottom Line/Personal,* August 1, 1995 and February 1, 1995.)

The Sands of Time

> Time flies (*Tempus fugit*).
> —Ovid

Philosophers and physicists argue about the true nature of time; for most of us it simply passes faster than we'd like.

Using Time

> Spilled water never returns to the cup.
> —Japanese Proverb

Our careers depend upon the way we use the time that is available to us with minimal waste. Time can usually be saved by eliminating waste and nonessentials. Of course, nonessentials aren't always wasteful, for people can often benefit from a little break or diversion. But when you're facing serious deadlines, focus on what contributes to your goal and what does not, and make up your mind just how much time you can afford to spare.

> Remember that time is money.
> —Benjamin Franklin

In Pasadena, actuary Sureka Garu used to save commuting time by driving to work at 7 A.M. "Over a period of two or three years I had to leave earlier and earlier, until I had to be on the road by 6 A.M. in order to make the same trip in less than an hour. So I moved closer to the city, where everything is more expensive. I estimate that it costs me close to $19,000 a year to save an hour and a half of commuting time a day. At 360 hours per year, that comes to about $53 an hour, and I figure my time is worth at least that much!"

Time is far more valuable than money; the way you spend, invest, and squander time will have a much greater influence on your career. According to Stanley Marcus (the former chairman of Nieman-Marcus), "The difference between being successful and not being successful depends on how you use your daily ration of 24 hours."

> Why kill time when you can employ it?
> —French Proverb

Preparation (Chapter 21) is universally one of the best investments of your time. Getting ready in advance helps to get it right, which means efficiency of time and effort. And getting it right the first time means not having to waste time doing it over.

Two lumberjacks were chopping wood. One worked almost without stopping, while the other took periodic breaks. Yet at the end of the day, the fellow who took the most breaks had a higher stack of wood. "I just can't understand it," the first woodcutter said. "You stopped to rest a lot more often than me, and you still managed to cut more wood than I did."

"You weren't watching me during my breaks," said the second man, "or you'd have seen me sharpening my ax."

Wasting Time

> I wasted time, and now doth time waste me.
> —William Shakespeare

What constitutes a waste of time? It's the things you do that don't contribute to your needs and goals. The hours that you fritter away on low priorities and self-indulgence or squander through inefficiency become the time you wish you had back to use over again. How do you keep from wasting time? By examining the ways you spend it, and by establishing priorities and schedules.

Meetings and conferences rank high on the list of time wasters. Although not all meetings are unproductive, they often have a way of becoming more important than the problems they are scheduled to resolve, generating more new meetings than ideas. Peter Drucker has said that managers shouldn't spend more than 25% of their time in meetings.

A cartoon in the *New Yorker* had two secretaries setting up a conference table. "Make sure you leave some of those small pads around the table," one of them said, "in case someone has an idea."

The Tactics of Time Management

> Time is the scarcest resource, and unless it is managed nothing else can be managed.
> —Peter F. Drucker

Time management is based upon *awareness* and *planning*. You need to be aware of how you actually use your time in order to manage it. And effective management, of course, requires careful planning. The ultimate objective of time management is to get things done on time.

Accounting for Your Time

> The first step toward saving time ..is to find out how you've been spending it.
> —William Ruchti

Most time management and efficiency experts recommend lists in charting and planning time-consuming activities—if you aren't sure where your time is going, you need to find this out. We recommend beginning with a diary of your activities. A daily log of everything that takes at least 15 minutes of your time can open your eyes to the time-consumers and wasters in your life. You'll have to do this for at least a week for it to be truly meaningful; and two weeks would be even better. Your first day's log might look something like this:

MONDAY	ACTIVITY	RATING	TIME
8:55-9:30	Coffee/reviewed day's schedule.	A	35
9:30-10:20	Made phone calls, scheduled appointments.	A	50
10:20-10:45	L.B. came by to discuss REM project.	C	25
10:45-11	Paperwork.	B	15
11:10-12:15	JAL meeting (began 10 minutes late).	B	65
12:15-12:35	Talked to Sal & Uri about JAL meeting.	C	20
12:45-1:25	Lunch at desk/read status reports.	A	40
1:30-3:45	Worked on sales budget. (Interruptions: Sal –10, R.T. –8, phone –10)	A	135 (–28)
3:45-4:30	Intended 15 min coffee-break, got into discussion w/head of HRIS.	C	45
4:45-6	Sales budget (need another 2/3 hours). (Interruptions: phone –5)	A	75 (–5)
6:15-6:30	Planned tomorrow's schedule.	A	15

Total: 520 (–33)   A: 350   B: 80   C: 90 (+33 on phone & interruptions)

Your daily log will illustrate how most of your time is spent, productively and otherwise. If this turned out to be a fairly typical day, you might consider:

- Leaving for work 30 to 45 minutes earlier;
- Shutting your office door (if you have one) during designated periods;
- Not answering your phone during designated periods;
- Delegating someone else to nonessential meetings, if possible.

Some people find it useful to extend their log to the entire day, including getting ready for and traveling to and from work, time spent after work (both business and personal), and weekends.

Tooling Up

> There is a world market for about five computers.
> —Thomas J. Watson, Sr. (founder and first president of IBM, in 1943)

Technology includes not only the latest computer systems but also the telephone, fax, and countless gadgets and services. If you are out of touch with the latest technologies, take a look at what your successful colleagues are using. Ask around, read some business or specialty journals, and find out what tools people in your profession are using to get and stay ahead of their competitors. You don't have to be an innovator to avail yourself of many of the resources that are available to you—there's plenty of information out there to clue you in once you make the effort to uncover it.

Controlling Your Time

> The best-laid schemes o'mice an' men,
> Gang aft a-gley,
> And leave us naught but grief and pain,
> For promised joy.
> —Robert Burns

Every minute spent in planning is likely to save minutes, if not hours, in accomplishing whatever you set out to do. Plan your weeks and months one day at a time: Prioritize, schedule, and then act.

> Devote 100% of your time to the critical issue.
> —Robert Townsend

Prioritizing (Chapter 9) is the first essential step in planning your activities. After all, it doesn't matter how much you accomplish if it isn't what you really need or want to do. Prioritizing means deciding on what you want to accomplish first, next, and so on. When you prioritize tasks, consider (1) the importance of the task, (2) when it needs to be done, and (3) how long it will take you to do it.

Priorities encourage us to decide *what* to spend our time on, and *why*, which helps us to sustain the effort. Commitment—a dedication to a cause or action— should be a thoughtful and deliberate process. Just as we would be committed to our priorities, we must take care not to commit our time and resources to pointless and misguided activities. Once you get started, it can take enormous discipline and honesty to recognize that you are committed to a wrong or losing effort, and to step back from it.

> How does a project get to be a year behind schedule?
> One day at a time.
> —Fred Brooks

Don't trust important dates to memory. Calendar-type appointment books are essential for keeping your schedule properly organized. Without recording times and dates, you risk double-scheduling (making plans to be in two places at the same time), leaving insufficient time to prepare for meetings and events, failing to take advantage of available time periods, or even forgetting appointments, follow-ups, and other items.

Clear potential obstacles from your path in advance rather than at the last minute. Consider your health, needs, and capabilities. Be as fair and reasonable with yourself as you are with others. And remember to take breaks from time to time to "sharpen your ax."

> The ultimate inspiration is the deadline.
> —Nolan Bushnell

A deadline is the natural transition from priority to schedule: The priority is established, the deadline is determined, and the task is scheduled. Deadlines lend an air of credibility to tasks that may otherwise slide until they become burdens or emergencies. They encourage planning and activity.

Multitasking is doing more than one thing at a time; reusing (batching, piggy-backing) means getting additional mileage from your time-consuming labor. This involves reducing duplication of effort and borrowing on past accomplishments. Examples may include taking out the trash when you go out to walk the dog, using past proposals and reports as the nucleus for new ones, and setting up multiple appointments on the same side of town.

> ..when a man knows he is to be hanged in a fortnight, it concentrates his mind wonderfully.
> —Samuel Johnson

Effective use of time requires concentration and practice. The more you plan and organize your time, the more efficiently you'll use it. Eventually your focus and efficiency will become second nature, and people will be asking you how on earth you find the time for all the things you do. When people ask us that question, we often answer, "It takes focus, and a little timing."

▼▼▼

CAREER BUSTER 15

THE MISUSE OF POWER CAN BURN MORE THAN YOUR FINGERS

..after you have once ridden behind a motorcycle escort, you are never the same again.
—Herbert H. Lehman (N.Y. State senator in 1950)

Lord John Emerich Edward Dalberg-Acton wrote that (absolute) power corrupts (absolutely); George Bernard Shaw believed that it was men who corrupted power, not the other way around. However you may choose to view this question, it seems to be the nature both of people and of power that they are rarely compatible.

There is no *absolute* power here on earth. What privilege we do enjoy is subject to the turns of fortune: Yesterday's allies and enemies, subordinates and superiors, are in flux and influenced by changes we may not control. The wisdom of never crossing someone who can hurt you is clouded by this uncertainty: How can you tell who may grow in stature and someday bear you a grudge? The safest answer is that the fewer people you treat badly, the less antagonism you are likely to encounter down the road. For every life is touched by forces it alone has set in motion.

Power is attained primarily through achievement, affiliation, and coercion. It is used to influence, control, and dominate. For many, power is a protective device that helps us to get by; to others it becomes its own objective. When Henry Kissinger referred to power as the "ultimate aphrodisiac," he was providing an insight into the personalities of power addicts throughout history. To them, as George Orwell wrote, "Power is not a means; it is an end."

What is power? It is usually defined as *the ability to do,* i.e., to decide what is to be done, and to control how it is done. The English word originates from the Latin *potere,* which implies ability (i.e., to take whatever action needed or desired). If we explore the word still further, we find its Indo-European root, *poti,* which means lord, master, and also husband. These linguistic, cultural, and psychological roots can help us better understand our confusion about power.

134

The significance of power to your career lies in how you use it to get what you want, and how you cope when it is directed against you. However you define power, its misuse is not limited to excess, but extends as well to naîveté in making power work for you, and defenselessness in the face of its use against you.

 ## CAREER SAVERS
The Art of Power
The Abuse of Power
Sources of Power
The Tactics of Power

The Art of Power

> The King of Heaven has bestowed on me the dominion of the world.
> —King Darius III (to Alexander the Great)

> Surrender ..and you shall see I know as well how to deal honorably with those who I conquer.
> —Alexander the Great (in response to King Darius III)

Perhaps the ultimate in human power was expressed in this exchange between two legendary rulers. Darius, as many before and since, sought to borrow leverage from a higher source; but Alexander had the means to call his bluff.

Planning the Game

> Conquering others requires force.
> Conquering oneself requires strength.
> —Lao-tsu (from the Tao Te Ching)

Asian philosophy and tradition view the work and leisure aspects of the individual as one: Our business, spiritual, and philosophic standards and practices all stem from a single inner core. In contrast, many Westerners attempt to segment these aspects, for example, by behaving differently (tougher or more passively) in competitive environments than at home. Since it is extremely difficult to excel at that which one is not, this method rarely earns sustained success. The more practical and enduring plan is to decide what we would like to be, and to practice being that in all we do.

Playing the Game

> Be bold in what you stand for and careful what you fall for.
> —Ruth Boorstin

Power addicts play the game throughout their waking hours and very likely in their dreams. They do so by attempting to control their interactions with everyone with whom they come in contact: service-people, neighbors, family, and at work with colleagues, subordi-nates, and even their own bosses. Many of them learned as children how to play one adult against another, developed their styles during their school years by pleasing teachers and fending off the local bul-lies (or by becoming bullies), and refined their brand of manipulative displays of strength or weakness.

Much of what occurs at work results from these little games of give and take. When you ask or are asked for favors; when you jock-ey for position; when you seek a raise, promotion, special assign-ment, or privilege; or when someone tries to get something from you, a power contest is in session. On the greater scale, your entire rela-tionship with a person or group of people may become a power game in which each encounter is a minor skirmish.

Understanding the Game

> Empowerment comes from widening your understanding of the kinds of power going on around you and from uncovering a wider spectrum of possibilities for embracing power.
> —James Hillman

The path to power lies in recognizing the options that are available to you. As Mr. Hillman suggests, the first step is to expand your con-cept of power, and then to practice using it. This means becoming aware of your options—the types of power that may suit your per-sonality, values, and circumstances. For example, you cannot apply the same leverage to your boss and colleagues as to members of your staff; and you may not be comfortable playing by uncharacteristi-cally harsh or tough tactics. Conversely, you may find that your usual stance does not work well with certain types, and that you need to vary your approach to break through.

Frank Gomez is a Senior V.P. at an American manufacturing firm in Guadalajara, Mexico. "Because of the way I was brought up," he confided to us, "I find it difficult to fire people unless I really dislike them. When we had to make extensive cuts in staff due to the devaluation of the peso, I brought in an experienced 'hatchet-man' from our Mexico City office to do the dirty work for me. That way I could do what had to be done without being directly blamed by those who were left. Eventually, when this hombre went back to his regular job, I was credited with getting rid of him."

The Abuse of Power

> The desire of power in excess caused the angels to fall ...
> —Francis Bacon

There are today and always have been people who use their power wisely and others who abuse its privilege. Some are better equipped to handle the intoxicating taste of power, while others fall quite easily into its corrupting influence. One of the problems with power in our corporations and institutions is that it is poorly understood. There are few if any courses or seminars on power, although we learn from early childhood to venerate great men and women. We equate power with wealth and privilege rather than responsibility and purpose. We learn from our role models how to acquire power instead of how to use it wisely.

The only practical reason for having power is to control. Seeking to acquire power that you don't need is a waste of time and energy. The pursuit of power can keep you from discovering and attaining more worthwhile and satisfying objectives. And then, having acquired this unneeded power, what do you do with it? Are you not tempted to test and exercise it?

Too much of anything is wasteful. An excess of power has no purpose other than itself. Turned inward, it fails to satisfy, and so it feeds the habit of trying to gain still more redundant power; directed outward, there is a high potential for abuse.

Force

> I'm gonna be so tough as mayor I'm gonna make Attila the Hun look like a faggot.
> —[Philadelphia police commissioner] Frank Rizzo (during his successful campaign for mayor in 1971)

Force is the imposition of one person's will over that of another person. When you use force, you make it clear that yours is the only view that counts, regardless of what the other person thinks. However, the use of force is often counterproductive. The majority of people react negatively to force: They may be coerced into submission, but with resentment and little willingness to perform at their best. The late Sewell Avery, who for decades reigned supreme as president of Montgomery Ward, is reputed to have forced over sixty-five vice presidents out of power ..for questioning his own infallibility. This game of musical chairs led to financial travails and difficulties in attracting talented managers.

Alternatives to Force

> The softest of stuff in the world
> Penetrates quickly the hardest.
> —The *Tao Te Ching* (from the *Book of Water*)

The lightest touch applied to the right place at the right time can motivate a landslide, which is to say that movement can be initiated and momentum built through an economy of effort. Usually, it is preferable to enlist the energy of others toward your goals. This means searching for the key to people's values and desires and using it to unlock their willing cooperation; since other people's needs are not identical to yours, the only way to satisfy them is to discover what they are.

Finesse is using the least of what you've got to get the most of what you want. It is the choice of those who have relatively little power and must maximize their available resources; and of those with power who are tired of having to exercise it every day. Finesse is prevalent among diplomats and equals, and people who prefer to reserve their power for when it is truly needed.

Empowerment is one of the buzzwords of the 90s. When you empower others to make decisions and take action, you enhance your own power by extension: The more power your subordinates hold, the more you own.

Sources of Power

> Make yourself the sort of man you want people to think you are.
> —Socrates

Power is derived from both personal and inherited sources.

Power Words

> People resort to violence when their words fail.
> —Chinese Proverb

Communicating what we wish to say depends on finding the right words to say it. Our thought processes rely on our use of language: Without the right terminology our thoughts cannot be well defined. We need clear words to form clear ideas. But *idea* words, like *power,* are interpreted and understood differently by nearly everyone.

Power can mean political influence, the ability to make financial decisions, or large muscles, depending on the audience. This ambiguity makes communication difficult and it leads to enormous frustration. Our institutions and corporations are bursting with the futility of the undefined dreams and unfulfilled careers of those who lack the power of communication, the words that would help them to identify first to themselves, and then to others, what they want.

The power of persuasion is the most efficient means of getting and keeping your way. By convincing other people to do what you want (and to refrain from doing what you do not want), you enlist their willing support and minimize potential resistance. Persuasion uses the charm of argument and manner to influence another person. Persuasiveness depends on good communication and interpersonal skills—it is said that if Winston Churchill had spoken German as well as English, he might have talked Hitler out of starting a war. Persuasive charm can substitute for credibility; if this were not true, we might have had a President Perot instead of Clinton.

Authority can derive from personal qualities like force, persuasion, and language; or it may come automatically with a title or office. Many vice presidents acquire power by coattailing into a post that far exceeded the level of their personal qualities and prior achievements. A few grew into their office and then into an even greater one. When you are hired, promoted, or elected to a position of authority, its power is on loan to you for as long as you remain. When you leave, the power you inherited by virtue of the office is gone, and you are left with a measure of the power you brought with you and what you were able to acquire in the meantime. The power of office is an opportunity to grow or to diminish. The man who sits upon the throne is king as long as kings remain in fashion and only until another takes his place.

The Tactics of Power

> The urge to save humanity is almost always a false-face
> for the urge to rule it.
> —Henry Louis Mencken

Michael Korda frequently expressed the thought that life is a game of power, the object being to know what you want and then to get it. He wrote that power is an "essential expression of our humanity," the primary motivation for us to work. He argued that our desire for even limited power is stronger than our desire for money. This thesis plays nicely into the hands of our employers, since it costs them less to offer power and prestige than higher salaries. Thus it may appeal to many companies to promote the allure of power over that of financial security.

Power Things

> The appearance of power is power; it is the art of making "big sticks" out of little twigs.
> —Laurence J. Peter

The objects of power proliferate in our modern world in the form of trendy clichés. We wear power ties at power lunches with power brokers; we take power trips in power automobiles and power boats (equipped with power brakes and power steering); we use power tools, read power books, learn power phrases; and we play power games with other power players. We buy into these symbols as if to swallow power from a magic cup and so enhance our images.

Power Image

> If [a man] is brusk in his manner, others will not cooperate.
> —I Ching: Book of Changes

Your body and your manner of presentation contribute to the image you project. A calm and firm appearance is more suggestive of power than a nervous aspect. The confidence of belonging where you are—anywhere—supports this functional illusion.

Michelle is a professional image consultant in Los Angeles. She helps her clients gain the edge by teaching them how to dress and groom themselves to best advantage. "You'd be surprised how little some of these high-powered business types understand about their image," she told us. "I take them shopping, get their hair trimmed, and show them how to make subtle adjustments to the way they walk, stand, sit, talk, and listen. When I'm finished with them, they're ready to take on the world!"

In face-to-face encounters, the firmest power image is usually the most composed: impassive immobility while others squirm and fidget; steady eyes and mouth, feet firmly planted before you; shoulders square. There are other techniques that can enhance your power image: Wait to hear what others have to say before offering your observations or opinions in a confident tone; wear a jacket when everybody else is in shirtsleeves; lower your voice at strategic times to compel your listeners to lean forward and strain to hear you. Offer only as much information about yourself and your ideas as necessary and withhold the rest: Knowledge is power, and what you give away serves only to empower your opponents. Envision (even if you don't play cards) the perfect poker face: quiet, unflinching confidence, and never a bead of sweat! This is how the power types play their games.

Leverage

> When water is applied to fire, the result is often steam.

Leverage is the use of your own power, or influence you borrow from another source, to get something done. It relies on the impression (real or illusory) of authority. This may be based on position, precedent, convincing data, or any form of information that the other person is likely to respect or fear. It may imply a risk of punishment, a promise of reward, insurmountable obstacles, or a path of least resistance.

Denial

> To avoid the responsibility of power, one simply denies having any.

Not all power seekers will admit to its pursuit. In fact, there is a tendency to deny the personal benefits of power by complaining about the responsibilities it brings:

"I have no time to myself .."
"I hardly ever get to spend time with my family."
"My health has suffered .."
"I rarely ever get a day off."

Clichés of denial are intended to negate the impression that these people enjoy the power they have worked so hard to get, or that it is worth having. This may stem from the idea that we shouldn't enjoy something as crass as power, or perhaps it is a means of convincing those around us not to envy or compete with us. On the other hand, if they really don't like what they're doing and wanted to spend more time with their spouses and children, they most likely would.

Information As Power

> The more one knows about a person, the greater one's power to destroy him.
> —Stanley I. Benn

The power of information is common knowledge, but the means of its control and use are largely ignored. Paradoxically, the recording and retrieval of the data on which managers and executives base many important decisions is commonly assigned to clerical and junior staff. This leaves open to question the accuracy and completeness of the data. If you ask a secretary who knows nothing about inventory for certain figures, he or she may not realize that stock depreciations, write-offs, and ordered items not yet received are also relevant to the bottom lines you need. If you're asking about product development costs, there may be information buried under other headings that only a project manager would know about. Data can be classified in a variety of creative manners. It follows that the reliability of your information may vary according to its source.

One of the most effective ways to win your point is to establish it on (what appears to be) solid information. If anyone tries to argue, you can pleasantly remind him or her that your position is based on fact, not opinion. And if you are the only one with total access to the relevant data, no one is likely to challenge you.

Indispensability

> All employees are dispensable, but some are more dispensable than others.

Like power, indispensability is a myth that can be grown and nurtured into a virtual reality. If you work toward making yourself very useful, others will rely on you. The objective is to provide a useful service without ever letting others discover that they can get along quite well without you.

For example, a secretary who knows where everything is and saves the boss a lot of time attains an aura of indispensability. To maintain this role, he should limit himself to short vacations (preferably a week, but no more than two weeks) during which his replacement is completely befuddled. If he is ever absent long enough to allow someone else to become fully oriented, the aura may evaporate. A manager who assumes some of the functions of the department head becomes indispensable by enabling her boss to spend more time on other priorities.

Attaining Power

> ..[power] is all around us; we have only to seize it. It does not lie beyond the everyday activities of our lives, but in them.
> —Michael Korda

Power rarely occurs by accident. To acquire power, you must desire and actively seek it. If you are not driven to power, if you are not attracted to its pursuit and license, you are not likely to attain it. As Don Juan taught to Carlos Castaneda: "There is no way to escape the *doing* of our world, so what a warrior does is to turn his world into his hunting ground. As a hunter, a warrior knows that the world is made to be *used*. So he uses every bit of it." And, in turn, is used.

▼▼▼

CAREER BUSTER 16

NEGLECT NETWORKING AT
YOUR OWN PERIL

> The fisherman casts his net and gathers the bounty of
> the sea.

In its simplest form, networking is the process of talking to people
to receive and share information. Its objective is to provide you
access to individuals and spheres of influence that may otherwise
be unavailable to you. Networking can be used to find a job, support
a business, and enhance a career.

Although widespread, networking is a poorly defined practice
that incorporates the best and worst of human tactics and behavior.
It used to be a more casual process: People called each other and got
together to chat about issues of mutual interest. They met the friends
and colleagues of their friends, and sometimes this led to a job lead
or a business arrangement. The formalization of networking as a
job-getting and career-enhancing function was the result of an increasingly competitive job market. Executives began to better understand the value of sharing information and contacts, and both recruiters and headhunters honed networking into an effective tool.

Some disgruntled executives speculate that networking is on its
way out: "...there's a backlash against networking because it's been
so overworked," claims the chairman of a major eastern outplace-
ment firm. "Many networking targets are growing increasingly reluctant to return calls." Others insist that networking is being elevated to a discipline and a hiring point in certain industries.
Networking specialist and author Ann Boe believes that networking
will be taught in business schools and corporate training classes. (In
fact, networking has for some time been taught in a number of major
universities.) Ms. Boe makes the point that networking skills help
service providers, such as hair stylists and stockbrokers, to bring
loyal customers and clients with them as they move from one employer to another.

The fact remains that networking is the vehicle by which the
overwhelming majority of jobs are found. Love it or hate it, your career will probably be influenced by your ability to network. Network-

ing is hard work and can be extremely time-consuming. Many would-be networkers grow frustrated and discouraged when their efforts seem unrewarded, and just give up. The rules of thumb are these: You've got to do it carefully, and you must persevere to make it work for you. There is definitely an art to networking, and there are specific tactics that can help you network successfully and productively.

CAREER SAVERS

The Art of Networking
The Goals of Networking
The Tactics of Networking
Electronic Networking

The Art of Networking

> Vain the ambition of kings
> Who seek by trophies and dead things
> To leave a living name behind,
> And weave but nets to catch the wind.
> —John Webster

Q: What is worse than spending an entire afternoon with an Internal Revenue auditor?
A: Spending an hour with a networker!

Over the past decade networking has inflated into near epidemic proportions. A lot of people are turned off by insistent would-be networkers who abuse their introductions and impose unfairly on their target's time. Poor networking practices are a handicap to those who would expand their horizons, and artless networkers make it yet more difficult for everyone else.

Some of the experts recommend cramming (they don't call it that) a lot of information about yourself—what you've done, where you've been, what you're capable of doing, and what you'd like to do—into even casual networking conversations and letters. We caution that what seems interesting and pertinent to you may be overkill to others. Clearly this is a difficult issue to evaluate, and so we offer two guidelines. First, try your pitch out on a close friend or family member to get a read on it, and try it on yourself ...what would be your reaction to someone who addressed you in a similar manner?

Second, when you're speaking with others, watch their reactions to you. Be sensitive to their attention level and body language.

Networking requires a sense of purpose, strong communication skills, time, dedicated effort, and a rock-solid ego. Add to this a pleasant manner and you're ready to begin. If your tool kit lacks any one of these elements, you are advised to make every effort to acquire it, or at least to compensate with a rather charming personality. Otherwise your quest may turn into an ordeal. The two primary objectives of networking are to acquire information and to establish personal contacts. Both of these are accomplished by talking and writing to people to let them know what you are looking for.

Information Networking

> Information is power; knowledge enables its productive use.

A Miami restaurant owner decided to make a regular practice of giving unwanted food to the homeless. This would be a humane way to dispose of perishables left over from the weekend, still perfectly edible, but no longer fresh enough to serve to his customers. He announced his plan to an elderly lady who regularly came by to ask for handouts and invited her to tell a few of her needy friends to come to the rear entrance of the restaurant at 2 o'clock on Monday afternoons. She told a couple of her friends, and they told a few of their friends. By noon on the following Monday, close to forty people were lined up in the alley—this was a particularly good restaurant, and the word had gotten around.

Used wisely, timely information can enable you to make good decisions and stay out of trouble. If you hear of a forthcoming opening and can find out who will be responsible for filling it, you may have a better shot at the job than another equally qualified candidate who hears about it later. You may even be able to win the prize before the requirement is posted, or at least position yourself on the inside track.

To gain information about a company or a profession, you talk to people who have personal experience in your area of interest. There is really no better way to find out what you want and need to know about a job or industry, aside from working in it yourself. People in positions you might like to be in are prime networking targets. They can give you inside information about what the job is really like, and help you to decide if it may be right for you. A note of caution: Don't limit yourself to a single source of information, but ask each person with whom you speak for a name at another company. Any one individual's view of an industry or company might be exaggerated or prejudiced, and the consensus you draw from several people is more likely to be reliable.

Contact Networking

> Networking has a life of its own. You put your energy
> out there, and even when you're not around, people
> respond to the echoes of that energy.
> —Howard Berelson

Like many artists, Howard Berelson depends on networking to have his name and work become better known among art dealers and collectors. He has a painting in the permanent collection of a museum not far from his Teaneck, New Jersey studio. Another artist, whose work was also displayed at that museum, convinced a private gallery owner to visit the museum to see her paintings. When the gallery owner came, he was more impressed with Berelson's style and asked the museum director to set up a meeting. This proved worthwhile for all three parties. "I was able to learn what he (the gallery owner) was looking for and gain an insight into his vision," Howard summarized. "Now that I understand the constraints to which he is subject, I can decide if I am able to meet them." For his part, the museum director was pleased to develop a closer relationship with the gallery owner.

Networking is the orchestration of a string of contacts into a harmony of purpose. Contact networking is used to gain access to specific individuals or to *types* of people. This may be done directly or via referral.

The idea is to convince your contact to introduce you or refer you to someone you want to know, or to people in a certain company or industry. The more people you meet, the more referrals they may help you make in turn. If possible, have your contact notify the person to whom they are referring you. Otherwise, you may find it helpful to address a brief note to the target to introduce yourself, identify the person who referred you, and mention why and when you plan to contact the target.

Often there is no other way to try to reach someone than by contacting them directly. This approach is more graceful when you are able to come up with a personal reason for the contact, e.g., "I read your article ..."; "I was interested in your quote ..."; "I am aware of your reputation in..." Next best is showing some knowledge of the person's company from a media reference or annual report. Not everyone is comfortable with this method of contact, but those who make the effort can sometimes achieve a great deal in a very short time.

> One such example is the energetic undergraduate at a state university in Ohio who was interested in public relations. He read up on the field, organized a game plan, and found the phone number of a major corporation in the local telephone directory. His first call was directed to the switchboard operator, from whom he obtained the correctly spelled name and title of the vice president of public relations. He then placed a call directly to the vice president, managed to get through to him, and scheduled a brief interview. The student did his homework on the company and drew up a list of insightful comments and questions. He refined his list with the help of an instructor. His preparation, enthusiasm, and positive attitude led the VP to extend the interview to several hours, and resulted in an internship the following year.

The Goals of Networking

> If you don't know where you're going, you might wind up someplace else.
> —Yogi Berra

The information you acquire and the contacts you make can be used to find a job, expand your business, or solidify your career. When you prepare to network, keep your objectives clearly in mind. At other times, be open to an opportunity to benefit a friend or member of your network.

Finding a Job

> It's not what you know ...

Networking is the primary vehicle for landing a job. According to the U.S. Department of Labor, networking plays a significant role in acquiring up to 80% of the positions obtained by professionals. People in the employment business say that this was probably true in 1990, and that today's ratio is closer to 60%. These figures suggest two obvious and important realities: that networking remains a vital tool in pursuing a successful career, and that the art of networking has grown as challenging and competitive as the job market itself. Although executive-level job-listing newsletters (such as *Exec-U-Net* and *NetShare*) and computerized job banks are expanding as alternatives, networking is not—despite what some disgruntled individuals insist—yet dead.

When you describe yourself to anyone who represents a potential job lead or who may speak to someone else about you, you need to offer a meaningful and easily recalled profile of your job-related attributes. Douglas B. Richardson, who runs a career management and executive consulting firm in Philadelphia, suggests that we characterize our "work identity" by dividing it into three groups: *technical skills, transferable abilities,* and *personal qualities.* By way of example, Richardson equates rocket science to technical skill (expertise), trouble-shooting to ability (experience and judgment), and creativity to personal qualities (temperament). An example might go something like this:

> I am an experienced inventory control manager {*skill*}. Most recently, I directed the installation of a new computerized system {*transferable ability*} by analyzing our order fulfillment patterns and revising our purchasing procedures {*qualities*}. Now I'm looking for an opportunity to be in charge of an entire merchandising operation {*objective*}.

Bear in mind that networking is not the same as interviewing for a job. If you arrange a networking meeting with a busy executive and try to turn it into a job interview, you are likely to meet with resentment. If you hope to obtain a job lead from someone, let them know this up front. Otherwise, stick to the prearranged agenda.

Expanding Your Business

> When Steve Jobs (founder of Apple Computer) was 12, he called Bill Hewlett (founder of Hewlett-Packard) to ask for some free parts.

Service providers like insurance sellers, stockbrokers, accountants, financial consultants, real estate agents, and beauticians are a sampling of people in careers that depend on developing a loyal client base. A hairdresser's value to a boutique is like that of a stockbroker's: attracting, serving, and maintaining loyal clients. Partnerships, raises, and promotions are based in large measure on this single talent; and networking, whether planned or word-of-mouth, is the major tool.

Solidifying Your Career.   Your ability to get along with people affects your progress in most organizations. This depends on your interpersonal and networking skills. Networking can help you forge solid relationships with management, colleagues, and subordinates by allowing you to get to know them better, and through an ongoing exchange of information and assistance. The more people in your office network, the more likely you are to hear about issues that affect your decisions and about corporate priorities and concerns that can help you do a better job (and stay out of trouble).

The Tactics of Networking

> ..never ever, no matter what else you do in your life, never sleep with anyone whose troubles are worse than your own.
> —attributed to Nelson Algren (by H.E.F. Donohue)

Networking skills can be an asset at any level of a career for:

- beginners seeking information on which to base a career decision or looking for contacts through whom to find a promising position;
- people trying to expand their business contacts and advance in their careers;
- senior workers and professionals in need of valid retirement options.

The trick is knowing where and how to invest your time and efforts wisely.

Which Nets to Work

> Knowledge is of two kinds: We know a subject ourselves, or we know where we can find information upon it.
> —Samuel Johnson

Hot networking begins with whomever you know who may have the power, knowledge, or ability to help you. Cold networking starts where you live, work, and spend time. Your hit list is likely to include most, if not all, of the following groups of people:

- Family, both immediate and extended
- Friends: people with whom you socialize
- Social colleagues: members of your clubs and religious group
- Professional colleagues: people with whom you work or used to work

- Academic colleagues: your alumni association, former classmates and teachers
- Service providers: doctors, dentists, accountants, insurance agents, stockbrokers, shopkeepers, hairdressers, service station mechanics, and so on
- People with whom you share a common (foreign) language, ethnic background, or concerns (such as parents', political, and women's issues)
- Neighbors

Your next source can be associations of which you are not a member but which may be available to you. Explore your local chamber of commerce, the service clubs in your community, your town or city hall, library, newspapers, and *Yellow Pages* for information about local businesses and activities, and the people who run them. If you have access to a computer, the networking world of cyberspace awaits you. When you feel ready for the challenge, you can follow up the referrals (the people to whom you have been referred from your original contacts), and perhaps take part in a formal networking group.

Allocating Time.   There's no way around the fact that networking is a time-consuming activity. Networking time must be allocated carefully—otherwise a busy person probably won't get around to it, and an undisciplined individual may waste time unproductively. An active networking agenda needs more time than simply renewing contacts. Maintain a list of people to be contacted; schedule a specific period of time each day, once or twice a week, or as often as needed, for phone calls. Plan to use at least one lunch a week to get together with certain individuals, and set a goal in keeping with your priorities: so many people to touch base with every week or month, so many new people to contact. Take advantage of spare minutes to make a call; pick up the phone instead of going outside for a cigarette, or call someone while enjoying a cup of coffee.

The "rules" of networking read much like any other interpersonal protocol:

Be ready. Put yourself in a networking frame of mind before calling a target or getting together with potential contacts. In face-to-face encounters, dress appropriately, and have business cards and other suitable materials with you. Prepare to discuss at least one topic of potential interest to the people you expect to meet.

> When Myer was getting started as a stockbroker in Austin, he always had a few details of timely market information ready to share with people he met at his athletic club. Of course, it was only public information readily available to anyone, but he had discovered that people in other businesses don't always have the time to read up on the market.

Be tactful. Some conversations justify giving out your card, others don't. Similarly, it may be appropriate to hand out copies of your résumé at a recruitment meeting but not at a social gathering. There is a vital distinction to be made between subtle, acceptably aggressive, and overbearing behavior.

> Myer made a point of never offering his card unless it was requested; it wasn't long before several club members were asking for two or three cards at a time, and the calls began to come.

Be discreet. Keep personal problems, gripes, and negative references to yourself—do you want to spend time listening to someone's else's complaints?

Be patient. Networks take time and effort to establish and maintain. A single contact may bear fruit almost immediately or years later— if at all. Look at everyone in your network as a potential career-saver, and use your conversations with them to practice being a better networker.

> When Myer relocated to Dallas, he kept track of the contacts he had made in Austin, even those with whom he had done no business. He regularly sent cards to a number of his former clubmates to acknowledge special occasions. One, who was pleasantly surprised to receive a card congratulating him on his marriage, told his bride about Myer in the presence of her father. The conversation led to a phone call to Dallas and a new client for Myer, who was viewed by the family as an old friend of the groom.

Be purposeful. Whether your reason for getting in touch with someone is to initiate a relationship that may help you down the line, or to ask for specific information or an introduction, every contact that you make should be motivated by a purpose.

Be clear. If you are vague about your objectives, no one will be able to help you.

Be creative. Look for opportunities to link the interests of other people to your own.

> Larry is the recruitment manager of an Atlanta office-temp agency. Walking past a bridal shop one morning, it occurred to him that a number of newly married women might be interested in part-time work. With this thought in mind, he entered the store and persuaded the owner to keep a stack of his cards on the counter next to the cash register. He reasoned that the cards might help her business by providing an interesting topic of conversation with her customers. He then designed a special card inviting newlyweds and others interested in part-time work to call him, and offered a $10 gift certificate to the bridal shop to any qualified candidate who came in for an interview. The owner of the store loved the idea and let Larry put up a small, attractively designed cardholder. The first three months alone, Larry's firm placed over a dozen temps from this one source.

Be positive. Your attitude colors people's enthusiasm for dealing with you. While some will be reluctant to give you the time of day no matter how you present yourself, most people enjoy talking to a pleasant, upbeat individual. A positive attitude sets your expectations toward success and promotes your credibility to others.

> A colleague of Myer's used to begin his calls to prospective clients with openers like, "I don't know if this will be of interest to you, but..." He is now employed as an assistant analyst with a retirement fund. By contrast, Myer greets the people he calls with the expectation of a profitable discussion: "I thought you would be interested in hearing about..."

Be sensitive to the other person's time constraints and interest in speaking with you. Focus your listening on reading irritation and impatience in people's voices; if they tell you (or sound like) they're busy, ask when might be a better time to call. Avoid wearing out the welcome mat. Remember, if someone feels that you are wasting their time, you're also wasting yours!

Be aware of the other person's values by listening carefully to what they say and how they say it. Some people are offended by what others find amusing, so you are advised to avoid the types of comments that may alienate you from your contact before getting to know them.

Be prepared. A little homework and planning enables you to refer to issues and details that are likely to interest your target *and to avoid those that aren't.*

> Myer has no personal interest in stamps. However, his brokerage firm receives letters from around the world, and he thought it was a pity to just throw them away. On a whim he began to collect the interesting looking stamps he received in a large brown envelope. Eventually, a prospective client mentioned in passing that her son was starting a stamp collection. Myer mailed the stamps to the mother of the young stamp collector with a friendly, handwritten note and gained a very appreciative client.

Be thoughtful. The serious networkers on your list are likely to have lists of their own. The best way to remain active in their networks is to provide them with useful information and contacts. Most people whom you have helped in any way will be willing to make an extra effort for you.

> Whenever Larry hears of someone who is getting married, he makes a point of recommending the bridal shop. "Tell Suzannah—she's the owner—that Larry sent you."

Be relevant. Avoid frivolous referrals. Just because you happened to meet a self-employed business owner, that doesn't necessarily make them a hot prospect to an acquaintance who sells disability insurance. Passing along inappropriate referrals or questionable information is a sure bridge burner.

Be reasonable. Don't ask for more than people are legally or ethically able to provide.

> When pressed by a client to recommend a stock, Myer tactfully reminds them that his role is to provide information and perspectives that can help them make informed decisions of their own.

Be organized. Unless you have a photographic memory, use a computer, Rolodex®, notebook, or other filing system that enables you to keep track of everyone you speak to. List their names, phone numbers, dates of contact, birthdays and other significant dates (excellent opportunities to send cards and call to keep in touch), your reasons for contacting them, information and referrals that you gave them or received from them, and similar details concerning these referrals.

> Myer has a networking database on his computer. Whenever a member of his network calls, he quickly accesses that person's file and uses it to make a thoughtful reference: "We haven't talked since you moved into your new house ..have you finished renovating the kitchen?" "Which college did your daughter decide to attend?" "Did your friend, Frank, get

the job with Aardvark Industries?" When he talks to someone for the
first time, he tries to learn a personal detail that can be tied to a date or
time period. His database automatically brings these dates to his
attention ten days before they occur, enabling him to send cards (or little
gifts) and plan calls with plenty of lead time.

Be responsive. Return phone calls promptly, offer what assistance
you can to those who are referred to you, and stick to any promises
you make. Everyone you help becomes a member of your network
and is likely to add you to theirs. Remember too that even entry-level
employees may have contacts of potential use to you.

Be courteous and pleasant. "Please" and "thank you" are still very
much in fashion, and their absence can be extremely annoying.

Be loyal to the members of your network. Speak well of them, and
be vigilant for ways to render service to them, whether they have
helped you in the past or not.

Be committed. Follow up on contacts and continue to expand your
network—if you're not in this for the long haul, don't even bother.

The pitfalls to be avoided can be summarized into a much
shorter list:

Never misrepresent the nature of a relationship, the purpose of your
contact, or your qualifications. Exaggerations and distortions, when
exposed, will cost you credibility.

Avoid risky topics like politics, religion and ethnicity, and sex. These
are among the most sensitive subjects to the greatest number of people. Even if you're sure that you and your target are in agreement on
one of these issues, you never know at what point your views may
go off in separate directions.

Getting Started

> Networking is a systematic approach to a random
> process.

Whenever you initiate a new contact, be sure to let your target know
your purpose. Identify the source of your referral—a mutual associate or acquaintance, a journal article or quote, a professional directory—and ask for an appointment of specified duration (usually

from 20 minutes to a half hour). Include just enough information about yourself to enable the other party to decide if they are interested in meeting you.

Suppose you are considering the posibility of working in the chemicals industry. When you speak to someone who may be in a position to help or inform you, you can simply tell them: "I'm exploring a career in chemicals. Can you refer me to anyone in the field?" When you write or call a potential contact, keep it simple, to the point, and respectful.

Maintaining Momentum. The hardest part of networking is getting started. Once you begin to make some headway it gets easier. If you stop, you'll have to get yourself going all over again. The only way to build and maintain a network is to systematically continue to expand your contact base while following up on earlier leads and suggestions.

Impromptu networking may also work for you if you are comfortable talking to acquaintences and strangers at social gatherings, in a plane or bus, or while on vacation. On occasion, a tactfully posed question may initiate a useful contact: *I'm looking for a tax accountant with experience in setting up trusts. Do you by any chance know one whom you could recommend?,* or *Do you happen to know anyone connected with the chemicals industry?*

Be prepared to hear a lot of variations of "Sorry, but ..." without getting discouraged, and then change the subject or just let it drop. If you click but once in fifty tries, you may have gained a lot with very little ventured. Whenever you establish a networking relationship with someone, be sure to follow up with them on live issues, and keep in touch from time to time even when there's nothing special cooking. This is the key to maintaining an active network.

Quid Pro Quo. When you ask for information or a referral, be prepared to offer something in return. After all, a person who helps you has every right to expect you to do the same for him or her someday. It may happen during the same conversation, a year later, or never, but you should be alert for an occasion to return the favor. Even better, take advantage of an opportunity to assist a fellow (or potential) networker before you need anything from them. A service rendered for someone else is money in the bank, even if you never spend it. It's a win-win situation: The other person benefits from your help and appreciates your effort on their behalf, and you feel good about yourself. When you've done someone a favor, file it away to memory. Avoid the temptation to bring it up. Reminding people of what you've done for them reduces a good deed into a bargaining chip; no one wants to feel indebted, and gratitude can quickly fade.

Electronic Networking

Many computer users enjoy the informality and faceless anonymity of cyberspace. Commercial online networking services like America Online, CompuServ, Delphi, GEnie, and Prodigy carry career-related SIGs (special interest groups), also known as boards, clubs, forums, and groups. You can read and (if you wish) respond to notices left by other networkers, leave your own notice to which thousands of SIG members can respond, and you can participate in a "real time" conference, interacting almost instantly with people all over the country and, indeed, the world.

Electronic networkers love to share information and opinions on anything at all, and queries as to the ups and downs of working in a particular industry or location are virtually guaranteed to elicit some enthusiastic responses. We've seen questions from students asking for advice on how to line up jobs, computer specialists seeking technical information, and unemployed cab drivers looking for better opportunities in other cities. There are also thousands of local groups that operate freestanding BBSs (bulletin board systems). You may find them listed in the magazine *Boardwatch* (800-933-6038), or through your computer dealer or library. *Online Access* is another journal listing BBSs and more general information on this brave new world. Caution: Online networking can be addictive!

▼▼▼

CAREER BUSTER 17

INDECISION GETS YOU NOWHERE

> In my view, he who goes ahead is always the one who wins.
> —Catherine the Great

From Catherine the Great to Oliver Wendell Holmes, the literature is rich with advice contrasting risk to circumspection. Some urge us to play it safe, others recommend prudent action, and a few throw caution to the winds. Which of these is best? Experience and common sense tell us that there are times when decisions need to be made and action taken, when indecision and inaction will be damaging. We also recognize the liability of impulsive, uninformed behavior. Clearly there is a balance needed between brash, self-defeating action and the paralysis of excessive caution.

Our objective here is to represent the different attitudes and factors involved in decision making, and the consequences of both taking and avoiding risks. Those who find themselves entrenched at either extreme are emphatically advised to read this chapter. They may find here the means and the encouragement to overcome their polarized positions and adapt to a more productive pattern.

CAREER SAVERS
The Art of Making Good Decisions
The Tactics of Taking Risks

The Art of Making Good Decisions

> Get it right or let it alone. The conclusion you jump to may be your own.
> —James Thurber

—but

> He that is overcautious will accomplish little.
> —Johann Von Schiller

158

Richard J. Stegemeier, of Unocal Corporation in Los Angeles, identifies decision makers as people who are "...willing to make tough decisions and stand by them." He adds that delegation of authority goes together with holding people accountable for their decisions and results. But how do we learn to differentiate between wise and poor decisions?

The process of making and avoiding decisions is based upon a balance of our goals, comfort zones, judgment, and habit. How important is the goal? What are the probabilities of success or failure, and the likely consequences of each? How much trouble must we suffer to achieve it? How do we *feel* about all this? How accustomed are we to making decisions of this kind?

Making a Decision

> There may be times when the best decision is to do nothing.
> —Ray Josephs

—but

> ...when the time for action has arrived, stop thinking and go in.
> —Napoleon Bonaparte

Decisions are made continuously throughout our days and lives. Some are fairly automatic, such as which TV program to watch; others, such as which restaurant to have dinner in, may require a few seconds or minutes of consideration. Major decisions take longer because the circumstances that influence them can be complex, and their potential consequences may bear heavily on our lives. Family, health, financial, and career choices are among the most important we are called upon to make. Although this book is oriented toward careers, the principles and mechanisms we address are generally applicable to most significant decisions.

The Elements of Decision Making

> We must as second best ...take the least of evils.
> —Aristotle

Decisions are either proactive or reactive, planned or impulsive. The formula for making a wise decision is to base it on a clear pur-

pose, consider the available options, evaluate potential consequences, and then decide as objectively as possible.

Always have a clear image of your objective (Chapter 9). The
purpose of a decision is to bring about a certain end; otherwise, why
do it? In our experience, most of the confusion that individuals and
groups experience about how best to do something is due to the uncertainty of their objectives.

> Don't be afraid when you have no other choice.
> —Yiddish Proverb

Harvard law professor emeritus Roger Fisher (*Beyond Machiavelli*)
and his coauthors analyze the perceived choices of decision makers
by potential consequences. They believe that experienced decision
makers tend to consider the following criteria before making important decisions:

1. Loss or gain of power
2. Exposure to criticism
3. Ability to explain and justify the decision
4. Impact on reputation
5. Impact on colleagues: Will it help or hurt them? Will they agree
   with it? Will they support me?
6. Impact on others (throughout the company or community): Will
   it be popular or unpopular? Who will support or resist it?
7. Policy: Is it consistent with my previous position? Does it set a
   (good/bad) precedent? Is it right or wrong?
8. Other options: What are the direct alternatives? What do I lose
   by delaying or withdrawing? What options will this open or
   close?

As a rule of thumb, the best decisions we make in our youth are
those that increase and enhance our future options. Later, as we mature, gain experience, and develop skills, we need to narrow down
some of these options into specific, well-defined goals. Otherwise,
we dissipate our energy, spin our wheels, and make little progress.

> At 30 years of age, Tom is mulling over a far-reaching choice: to pursue a
> promising technical career, to pursue the uncertainties of management, or
> to obtain a doctorate degree and enter academia. He recognizes that the
> technical arena limits his possibilities of climbing the company ladder; to

significantly increase his income, he would eventually have to become a
private consultant. Management offers greater corporate career
opportunities, but Tom isn't sure he likes or would excel at this. The
atmosphere and environment of academia (his father's milieu) is appealing
and would enable him to do some private consulting on the side.
However, this would require a PhD, which means years of evening classes.

We suggested to Tom that he attempt to run a project or two to
test the waters as a manager, and we asked him about the value of the
classes per se—would they be valuable to him only if he decided to
complete his PhD, or also in his corporate life? At this stage of Tom's
career, he loses nothing by trying his hand at management while taking
classes toward a possible graduate degree ..except, perhaps, a little
sleep. The expense of time and energy may demand a sacrifice of leisure
time and a few luxuries, but what an investment in his future!

Many people use charts to weigh the elements that can influence a
decision, and to contrast the likely outcomes of a pro or con position. For example:

Probable Consequences of Taking a Position on the XYZ Issue:

IF I AGREE:	IF I DISAGREE:
– I'll be criticized.	+ I'll be safe.
– I'll lose power.	+ I maintain my power.
– My budget may be cut.	+ I have nothing to lose.
– I give up the chance to gain something better.	+ I may be able to get something better later on.
but:	
+ The head of HR will become my ally.	– My staff will be disillusioned.
+ I gain exposure.	– I may be labeled as a wimp.

It's easy to be brave when far away from danger.
—Aesop

Anxiety can inhibit clear thinking. It alters the rational and evaluative processes that go into good decision making, often leading to
poor decisions and regrettable results. Pressure mounts when you
must make a decision by a certain deadline: The closer the cutoff
time, the more intense the pressure.

Careful planning and realistic scheduling help to reduce pressure. *The bottom line is for you—not someone else or random circumstances—to control the schedule.* When a deadline is imposed on you, try to step back from the situation to evaluate it unemotionally. Although this can be difficult to do at times, practicing these simple steps will serve you well over the long run. Mark H. McCormack (*What They Don't Teach You at Harvard Business School*) recommends that when you're faced with a crisis, you should not react immediately. Take a little time to think about it … then take your time to evaluate and consider options, alternatives, and consequences.

Avoiding a Decision

> Politics is the art of postponing decisions until they are no longer relevant.
> —Henri Queuille (former premier of France)

—but

> If you let decisions be made for you, you'll be trampled.
> —Betsy White

James I. Milner, Sr., is the founder of a Lexington, Kentucky electrical company. Milner believes that "…leaders are not afraid to make a decision." He speaks of the self-confidence that comes of an acquired knowledge based on education and experience. Of course, not all decisions must or should be made immediately; some can be postponed or avoided altogether. Let's look at these two options.

The best reason for delaying a decision is if the additional time will improve your chances for success; the very worst time to postpone one is if a delay is likely to exacerbate a situation. Many decisions are facilitated with better information and preparation. However, problems are easier to resolve than crises, and they have a way of festering when left alone. Ironically, people who avoid decisions lead risky lives. It's one thing to seek to minimize the effects of change, cling to familiar patterns, and avoid the hazards of unneeded risks. But avoidance of necessary, and timely, decisions leaves your fate in other hands or up to random factors out of your control.

The Tactics of Taking Risks

> Our whole way of life today is dedicated to the removal
> of risk.
> —Shirley Temple Black

—but

> Unless you enter the tiger's den, you cannot take her
> cubs.
> —Japanese Proverb

Goals cannot be pursued entirely without risk, nor can all risks be
clearly calculated. Successful people learn which risks are worth taking, and which to leave untouched.

Risks are based on reason, principles, and intuition. First, you
do your best to assess the situation: What must be done to bring
about a certain end, and is it worth the effort? This is a straightforward evaluation of cost versus potential gain. Principles invoke a
sense of right and wrong: Is this course of action consistent with
your beliefs? Can you live with the nature and result of your actions?
Instinct, which relies heavily on both reason and principles, provides
a sense of whether the risk *feels* like a good or bad idea. Rarely does
something that feels wrong turn out right.

> Be willing to take personal risks for the attainment of a
> worthwhile vision.
> —William T. Esrey

Success requires risk. We can't always play it safe if we want to play
to win in life. Otherwise we may be tempted to settle for nothing more
than a basic, minimal competence in what we do, at best. When you
consider making your move, always weigh the likely benefits against
the costs, and try to calculate the odds on both sides. If the payoff and
the probability of succeeding do not justify the risk, or if the potential
consequences could be damaging, it's probably the wrong risk.

Fear

> No passion so effectively robs the mind of all its power
> of acting and reasoning as fear.
> —Edmund Burke

—but

▼▼▼
Always do what you are afraid to do.
—Ralph Waldo Emerson

Fear of risk is fear of failing. It is a handicap that can inhibit your ability to function productively by making you unwilling to take reasonable and necessary chances. If you are locked into a pattern of inaction, an understanding of the process may help you to break out. Fear promotes useless, often dishonest activity, and paralysis. The best way to overcome your fear of risk is through analysis and reconditioning. An objective evaluation (see *Calculating Risks* later in this chapter) can take the magic out of risk by setting forth likely scenarios and outcomes. Consider the probable result of a certain action: What will happen if you do (don't do) it? What have you got to lose by taking or avoiding the risk? Is the threat of harm or loss realistic or exaggerated? Specifically what are you afraid of—can you define the nature of your fear?

In many corporate and public service environments, mistakes are punished with censure, embarrassment, or material penalties to a degree that discourages entrepreneurship and risk. People are afraid to hazard the impression of an error and go to great length to avoid the possibility of looking bad. A typical example is found among workers who handle quantities of cash, such as bank tellers, postal office workers, and toll collectors. When supervisors and managers harshly discipline their workers for even minor mistakes, service slows dramatically: The errors are often reduced, but at the cost of efficient service to customers.

The only way to avoid all risk is to do nothing ..and that doesn't really work, because people who sit in the middle of the road eventually get run over. Results are affected not only by our actions, but also by our lack of action. Failure to act can be more reprehensible than an honest attempt to make things right, especially if they go wrong. Freezing in the line of fire wins no battles or respect. If you are immobilized by fear when confronted with a crisis, it's time to reprogram your behavior by learning to take reasonable risks. The first step is to raise the level of your confidence.

The flip side of paralysis is overly aggressive behavior that leads to a collision with disaster. When urgent action must be taken, it doesn't mean that you should lower your head and push blindly ahead into the unknown. If you go too far in the wrong direction, you may be worse off than before and beyond the possibility of a correction.

Courage

> Fortune favors the brave.
> —Virgil

Courage is the ability to confront, control, and, when necessary, overcome your fears. A positive self-image helps you to act with courage because there is an expectation of succeeding; a lack of confidence promotes pessimistic thinking and an increased likelihood of failure. Ronald G. Assaf, chairman of a Deerfield Beach, Florida, electronics company, says that courage "..at its most basic, means the ability to make a decision and stick with it." Most often, courage stands for doing what you believe is right despite possible embarrassment and inconvenience.

When it comes to assuming and acknowledging responsibility, there is no middle ground: Either you are accountable, or you're not. Denying or attempting to mitigate ownership of obligations and results is lame and unconvincing. The advantage of owning up to your responsibilities early on is that you will, of necessity, be more committed to a successful effort. You can plan, assemble your resources, and enlist whatever help may be available.

Once your goals and priorities have been determined, you need a sincere commitment to sustain your efforts. Commitment helps to overcome problems, to maximize opportunities, and to uncover and develop latent talents. It also creates an atmosphere of credibility and optimism among those with whom you share your tasks.

Resisting Change

> ..every risk involves the threat of change and loss.
> —Richard Anderson

The threat of change invokes a fear of failure: Am I capable of learning new tricks? Am I up to the task? Will I be able to adapt to new conditions (as well as my peers), or will my inadequacies stand out? Will I sink or swim? Here you need to remind yourself that change isn't always an option, but a natural and inevitable force to be reckoned with. The risk of opposing or ignoring change is that it may occur in spite of you, and in ways controlled by others.

Calculating Risks

> You can and you can't,
> You will and you won't;
> You're darned if you do,
> And damned if you don't.
> —(based on the limerick by Lorenzo Dow)

Successful people take chances and, inevitably, make mistakes. For the most part, their errors are more than offset by their achievements. Without risk there is little opportunity for gain. You can overcome, or at least reduce, your fear of taking risks in two interrelated ways: increase your self-confidence, and recondition your behavior. Each of these activities will reinforce the other into an upward spiral of accomplishment.

> They say you can't always do it, but sometimes it doesn't always work.
> —Casey Stengel

—but

> We will either find a way or make one.
> —Hannibal

Make a list of the possible consequences of a risky project, i.e., the very worst that can happen if all goes wrong. It often helps to face the bogeyman in his lair rather than to imagine untold horrors. Be realistic—if necessary, get someone else's opinion to verify your own.

Next, note the circumstances likely to influence the outcome, pro and con, in separate columns. Do the odds appear heavily weighted toward the success or failure of this endeavor? How much effort will it take? Do you have the skills, experience, and resources to pull it off? Then write down the rewards if things turn out well and compare them to the potential negatives. Does the reward justify the risk?

Suppose you received a new job offer, one that promised a much better salary and career potential. To accept it, you must leave your current employer, where your career growth has been unexciting but steady. The new position would have greater risks along with increased responsibilities, and you're not sure that you can cut it. If it works out, you'll have made the right choice by accepting it;

if not, you're worse off than before. What should you do? The first step might be to create a list of pro's and con's on which to base your decision. Begin with a comparison between the positive attributes of your existing job and the new one. The following examples are intended only as simple outlines of the issues you may wish to consider:

Positives

OLD JOB	NEW JOB
current salary: $45K	entry salary: $58K
probable salary in: —1 year: $48K —5 years: $75K	possible salary in: —1 year: $65K —5 years: $90 to $100K
career potential: department manager	division VP
career options: limited	greater
personal growth: steady	unlimited
personal satisfaction: modest	unlimited

Then compare the negative aspects of each:

Negatives

OLD JOB	NEW JOB
chance of failing: minimal	higher, but not probable
requirements (time and effort): modest	higher
risk of losing job: —short term: low —5 years: unknown	—higher, but not great —unknown
worst case scenario: —short term: slow progress —5 years: unknown	—lose job, look for new one —unknown

Now list the additional factors that will influence your decision:

Other Factors

QUESTIONS	ANSWERS
Am I sufficiently qualified?	
—skills	—need to improve presentations
—experience	—no, but I can develop quickly
—talent	—they think so, and so do I
Am I willing to make the effort and sacrifices needed to succeed?	Yes.
Am I willing to deal with the possibility of failure?	If I want to get anywhere in life, I've got to take some chances and to find out about myself.
If I get fired:	
—how long is it likely to take me to find a new job?	—3-6 months
—can I afford to support myself in the meantime?	—yes—over 4 months would be tough, but I can survive
Is it worth the risk?	I deserve the chance!

Whether or not these specific elements and conditions are relevant to you and your circumstances, this approach can help you to weigh the issues that may affect a risk decision.

> Lady Godiva put everything she had on a horse.
> —William Claude (W.C.) Fields

Start with little risks that have only minor downsides and avoid anything that could cause you real damage. Knowing in advance that the worst that can happen isn't a big deal helps to keep you calm. Proposing a modest idea at work can increase the stakes of winning without great risk; if you believe that you have earned a raise or a promotion, what would you have to lose by speaking to your boss about it? The main idea is to try something you have been unwilling or reluctant to assay in the past.

Do your homework (Chapter 21) thoroughly to increase your chances of success. Seat-of-the-pants launches may be okay for people who have already achieved a measure of success in this manner, but not for Risk-Taking 101. Apply the notes you took during the analysis and use them to plan your moves. Track your progress, obstacles, and any changes that must be added to the equation. Solid preparation will contribute as much to your confidence as to your goal.

> Miracles sometimes occur, but one has to work terribly hard for them.
> —Chaim Weizmann

The odds of winning millions of dollars in a lottery are less than getting run over by a car or truck ..so don't bet your future on it. Although there is a time for patience, careers are made primarily through well-directed effort. *Survival of the fittest* is nature's way of rewarding those who make the effort, and culling those who don't.

Give yourself a pat on the back for making the attempt, smile at yourself for your progress, congratulate yourself for your success, and forgive yourself if things don't go exactly as expected. Recognize what you did right, how you might have done better, and the fact that you took a risk!

When the initial risk project has been completed, begin planning another just as soon as you can think of one. Each attempt, and every positive result, will help to reinforce your new habit pattern. As your confidence increases, so can the level of your risks.

Betting the Company

> He who fails to act must succumb.
> —Paul von Hindenburg

The difference between accepting a challenge and rising to the bait is *calculation*: Whereas the calculated risk takes many factors into account, the fish leaps to grab the promise of reward and glory without regard for probability of success, cost, and potential loss. The territory in between is gray, but then, the greatest, most courageous victories are usually won at the cost of the most infamous defeats.

> Viscount Horatio Nelson is remembered for his role in the British victory over the Spanish off Cape St. Vincent in 1797. When the admiral in charge of the British fleet decided to cease fighting, Nelson was convinced it was the right moment to attack. So Nelson turned his blind eye (lost in an earlier battle) to the admiral's signals and led the way to an audacious victory. The risk to his career was great, but fortune smiled upon the Englishman and rewarded him with favor for his boldness.

Avoiding Bad Risks

> As far as I'm concerned, nothing is worth going broke
> for.
> —Warren Avis

—but

> Fortune is not on the side of the faint-hearted.
> —Sophocles

The *Law of Unintended Consequences* contends that every action has consequences that were neither foreseen nor intended. This "law" is used by politicians, theorists, and other self-styled experts to argue against policies with which they happen to disagree. For example, Irving Kristol states that government regulations always have unintended consequences, and the importance of these consequences outweighs the intended consequences (Daniel Seligman, *Fortune*, May 29, 1995). We may conclude from this that since not all government regulations (e.g., income taxes, speed limits, and punishment for criminal acts) can be totally eliminated, we should do away with the ones that we don't like! On the other hand, a non-action is still a form of action, with consequences as real and unpredictable as any other. Lee Iacocca summed it up best when he said, "Every business and every product has risks. You can't get around it."

> ..Put all your eggs in one basket and—watch that basket.
> —Mark Twain

At every stage of your career avoid unnecessary, unjustified, and foolish risks. Keep the odds in your favor by selecting only those with a reasonable chance of success, that are justified by the reward, and where an unfavorable outcome won't cost you more than you can afford. There is a fine line between having the courage to do what others won't and living on the edge.

According to *The Times of London*, Salman Rushdie, the Anglo-Indian who lives under the Iranian threat of *fatwa* (sentence of death) for authoring *The Satanic Verses*, was recently seen at a book party dancing to the Bee Gees tune, *Stayin' Alive*.

Making Adjustments

> Innovations never happen as planned.
> —Gifford Pinchot III

—but

> All life is an experiment.
> —Oliver Wendell Holmes, Jr.

Sports have replaced war as the major source of metaphors in modern English. In competitive sports, the individual or team that is losing must either raise the level of performance, change tactics, or hope for a miracle. Those that are able to make the necessary adjustments often succeed in turning things around; the ones that obstinately stick to an unsuccessful strategy generally lose. Whether you are on the court or in the office, know where to draw the line between admirable persistence and stubbornness. Stick to your game plan long enough to give it—and you—a chance to be successful. But when it becomes clear that your strategy simply isn't working, look for ways to modify and improve the plan before it is too late.

CAREER BUSTER 18

TURNING DOWN A TOUGH ASSIGNMENT CAN TURN OFF THE BRASS

The buck stops here.
—Harry S. Truman

In Chapter 5, we discussed the advantages of being proactive in your work environment. Nowhere is this more evident than in dealing with the difficult and undesirable tasks that may be assigned to you, the ones for which you may earn little credit even if you get them right. In these situations it is essential that you seize the initiative so as to exercise the maximum control possible over the activities that are likely to determine the success or failure of your career.

When you must react to circumstances that are already in motion, you need to know what cards to play and how to exercise your options. Even if the hot potato is already in your lap, there may still be ways to minimize, if not eliminate, the pain. Which is better: a good offense, or a good defense? We choose offense, because as long as you keep running with the ball your defense is off the field. However, you must still be ready to protect your turf whether by direct resistance or more subtle maneuvers. And in both cases, you need to be mindful of the reasons for and the probable consequences of your actions.

CAREER SAVERS

The Art of Initiative
The Tactics of Avoidance

The Art of Initiative

..I do without being commanded ...
—Aristotle

The advantage of initiative is that you get the pick of the litter, the most interesting and rewarding projects. You become known as a cooperative worker, a team player, and an asset; and your efforts are more apt to be appreciated than those of your coddled colleagues. As an added bonus, fewer of the dull and nasty tasks that no one wants will be assigned to you.

Volunteering

> If a man will begin with certainties, he shall end in doubt; but if he will be content to begin with doubts, he shall end in certainties.
> —Francis Bacon

The old military maxim, "Never volunteer for anything," misses the point. Earning a reputation for shirking your fair share of the load leaves you at the mercy of decision makers who are likely to dump on you the most disagreeable and least appreciated chores. Whether and when to volunteer depend on how the job may serve your best interests.

> "When important things need doing, I always assign them to my best people," says hospital administrator Blaise M. of Tulsa, Oklahoma. "I save the garbage jobs for the lazy, uncooperative types—the ones who bitch and gripe no matter what you give them to do."

Criteria

> 'Yes' I answered you last night;
> 'No,' this morning, sir, I say:
> Colors seen by candlelight
> Will not look the same by day.
> —Elizabeth Barrett Browning

The major considerations in deciding whether or not to volunteer for a particular task are its importance to your boss and your ability and willingness to do it well. It is unwise to volunteer for something you are unqualified to accomplish, much less a job that's likely to go unnoticed and unappreciated.

> It's the sizzle that sells the steak and not the cow,
> although the cow is, of course, mighty important.
> —Elmer Wheeler

You need to know what your employer's priorities are if you want to get ahead in the company. It usually isn't too difficult to find this out, although it may take an effort to recognize them. Remember that everyone, from the highest executive to the lowest-paid employee, has his or her own perspective. Be aware that your supervisor (and her supervisor, and so on up the ladder) may see things differently from one another and from you. Unless you happen to read minds, the next best way to discover what's important to people is to ask and listen carefully to what they say.

> While in his manager's office, Charlie overheard him tell someone on the phone that he was looking for a bilingual secretary with good shorthand and telephone skills. Charlie, who is himself bilingual, volunteered to call a few personnel agencies and screen the applicants. His boss was delighted to have this time-consuming task taken care of, and he readily approved Charlie's final recommendation.

Before assuming an optional task, assess whether you have the tools to accomplish it with competence and in a timely manner. Also take into account your other responsibilities to be sure they won't be negatively impacted. If you lack the skill, knowledge, experience, resources, time, or other key ingredients, back off. Leave it for someone else, or suggest a collaboration that covers all the bases.

> For unto whomsoever much is given, of him shall be
> much required; and to whom men have committed much,
> of him they will ask the more.
> —*The Holy Bible* (Luke)

The effort it takes to do a good job isn't a whole lot more than what you would expend on mediocrity. Whether it's your normal work or something for which you've volunteered, always do it as well as you can. If your work is known to be minimal and shoddy, you won't often be entrusted with important tasks. After all, your boss is also judged to some extent by the quality of *your* work, and so the most critical and visible assignments will be handed to the best workers. Naturally, it pays to make an even greater effort on the special or highly visible projects that may be seen by a wider audience.

The more your company pays you, the more time and resources they invest in you, and the more responsibility they entrust to you, the more they will expect of you. This is the essence of their commitment to you and yours to them. It helps when your personal career goals are in synch with those of your employer: You learn and grow while contributing toward their objectives. Some discrepancies are tolerable, as long as you are both playing on the same field. When their expectations and yours are too far out of harmony to coexist, a change or redefinition is needed.

> The great business of life is to be, to do, to do without,
> and to depart.
> —John, Viscount Morley of Blackburn

Just as you enjoy the prerogative of pursuing your own career path, your company has a right to expect you to honor your commitment to them as long as you remain in their employ. Without commitment you will find it difficult to work productively. This may call for modifications to your responsibilities or a change of venue.

Responsibility

> Responsibility is the first step in responsibility.
> —William Edward Burghardt DuBois

We hear more and more people shouting and instigating for empowerment these days. Everyone seems to want privilege and respect; but these qualities cannot be given—they must be earned and paid for by accomplishment and responsibility.

> Civilizations, I believe, come to birth and proceed to
> grow by successfully responding to successive challenges.
> —Arnold Toynbee

The urgency and importance of a job aren't always related to its degree of difficulty. Still, easy tasks are rarely valued highly enough to become critical, and you can expect most important assignments to present some challenge. If you want to be valued and depended on, you must be prepared to roll up your sleeves and do what most of the other employees aren't willing to do. When you assume responsibility, you are accepting a new challenge.

> You're either part of the solution or part of the problem.
> —Leroy Eldridge Cleaver

Whatever your line of work, chances are your boss is looking for solutions to a number of problems. If you help to resolve some of these problems, you become an asset: The more solutions you provide, the greater the asset you represent.

Connecticut human resources director Madeline Kirby agrees wholeheartedly: "Most of my staff seem to be preoccupied with their own concerns. When someone takes the trouble to ask about some of the things I'm trying to deal with, I'm always happy for the chance to use them as a sounding board. And if they actually come up with a solution to one of my problems, their stock goes way up in my book!"

Managers and supervisors are always seeking people to whom they can turn for perspective and assistance. The more you can get them to rely on you, the better your position to assume added responsibility and privilege.

> Always fall in with what you're asked to accept. Take what is given, and make it over your way.
> —Robert Frost

As your responsibilities and privileges grow, so does your ability to influence your working environment. Providing solutions to other people's problems is a solid stride in the right direction. The next step is to identify problems or potential improvements that haven't been defined by anybody else, and to resolve them. Although flagging problems is itself a useful function, it is better to be associated with good news than bad. So think of this as a package deal, and keep the problem under wraps until you've thought out one or more alternative solutions.

> Russ Bartkowski, who runs a dry-cleaning chain in Oregon, believes that "The way to find solutions is to look for them. Most people know how to get out of the rain, but the guy who came up with the umbrella had a better idea."

The Tactics of Avoidance

> I took to my heels as fast as I could.
> —Terrence (Publius Terentius Afer)

Let's face it: Some assignments are a lot less interesting and rewarding than others. For the sake of your career, it makes sense to orient yourself toward the plums and away from the dogs. If you haven't taken the initiative to entrench yourself within the areas of your own choosing, you may find it useful to acquaint yourself with a few old-fashioned avoidance tactics.

Avoiding

> ...there is nothing more debasing than the work of those who do well what is not worth doing at all.
> —Gore Vidal

No matter how good and prideful a worker you are, some jobs do not inspire your best effort. It might be better to avoid them, if you can. Be on the lookout for jobs you wish to avoid, and stay abreast of impending projects with which you'd like to be involved. Also try to keep track of what your colleagues are doing, their talents and weaknesses, and their status with the boss. When you are confronted with an undesired chore, you may be able to persuade your boss that someone else is better suited to it than you, especially if you can make a case that they are less busy.

> Never do today what you can put off until tomorrow.
> —William Brighty Rands (Matthew Browne)

If you can legitimately delay beginning an ugly task, your boss may decide to assign it to someone who is immediately available. The operative word is *legitimately*, or you may be labeled as an unproductive malingerer. It may be possible to prolong your involvement with an existing project, cash in a couple of comp days to visit a sick aunt, or remind the boss that you have a planned vacation coming up which would delay the task's completion.

Between avoidance and refusal lies the compromise, the tactic of accepting within constraints and limitations. You may be able to restrict your obligation with mitigating statements like, "I'll be glad to do this for you, as long as I'm relieved from doing that"; "I'll get as much of it done as possible, as long as you don't expect me to finish it by that date"; "Since there's no way I can possibly get this done on time by myself, can I have Fred and Dagmar help me?" or "Must all of this be done by that date, or can part of it be done in a second phase?"

Refusing

> Do what thy manhood bids thee do, from none but self
> expect applause;
> He noblest lives and noblest dies who makes and keeps
> his self-made laws.
> —Sir Richard Francis Burton

The very last line of defense is to decline as tactfully and gracefully as you can. Italian writer Ignazio Silone (*Secondo Tranquilli*) suggests that "Liberty is the possibility of doubting, the possibility of making a mistake, the possibility of searching and experimenting, the possibility of saying 'No' to any authority..." The philosopher Epictetus advises us to "...do what you have to do." And Japanese novelist Dazai Osamu (Tsushima Shuji) laments, "My unhappiness was the unhappiness of a person who could not say no." There are, however, many ways of saying "no" without using the N word.

Within reason, you have the right to refuse inappropriate work that isn't part of your job description. Unfortunately, simply refusing on these grounds will earn you indelible black marks with your employer. If you feel that you are unable or unqualified to do what's being asked of you, it is reasonable to ask out or to request additional assistance. For example: "Carlotta may be better qualified than me to do this, and I know she has some open time on her schedule," is preferable to "I don't want to do it," or "Why do I always get stuck with the lousy jobs?" For that matter, William Tecumseh Sherman's well-known statement, "I will not accept if nominated and will not serve if elected," could have been more tactfully worded as, "I respectfully decline consideration for nomination as I would, regrettably, be unable to serve."

Overcoming Resistance

> I'll make him an offer he can't refuse.
> —Mario Puzo

If someone else is trying to worm out of an assignment that you want them to do, a little preparation (Chapter 21) can serve to nail them neatly into place. Finding out about their current duties and scheduling, for example, can reduce their possible excuses.

"When I have an unpleasant job to give someone," says Alabama manufacturing foreman Joe Chayevsky, "I try to set it up so that the guy has no way of ducking out. What I do is call him into my office and start off neutral, you know, like 'How are things going,' and so on. Then I say, 'I've got a problem, and I need your help.' I explain what needs to be done, put my hand on his shoulder, look him right in the eye, and tell him, 'I can always count on you, I know you won't let me down,' and there it is."

Lois Necker, a northern California investment broker, prefers the impersonal approach. "I tell my people, 'We have a very tight schedule and too little staff to get it all done, so we're all going to have to roll up our sleeves and pitch in. This is your assignment, and it must be done by this date. If you anticipate any problems in getting it done on time, write up a report explaining exactly what the problem is, and I'll review it and pass it along to the steering committee.' Well, no one likes to write reports, and they sure don't want to get their names brought up before the steering committee, so I get very few complaints."

CAREER BUSTER 19

REFUSE RELOCATION AND
GET LEFT OUT IN THE COLD

..the whole creation moves.
—Alfred, Lord Tennyson

There are many reasons for relocating. Usually it is your company or a potential employer that asks you to move. Or the move may be voluntary, to a preferred locale. Some moves are "permanent," that is to say, with no return or future move planned. Others are for a specified or limited period of time, as with most foreign assignments and study programs.

Relocation means different things at the beginning, middle, and toward the end of your career. If you have a working spouse and children in school, you may not want to pull up roots too often. Also, it can be risky to relocate to a place where it would be difficult to find a new job if you were to lose the one that sent you there. In some companies and professions, relocating at least once or twice is considered normal and necessary. Many sales positions are based away from the company's headquarters, and upper management positions may require a thorough familiarity with distant client bases and manufacturing facilities.

There is an art to relocation that consists of blending in with different habits and cultures; and there are ways to use relocation to your advantage without getting left out in the cold. As transportation and communication links continue to proliferate around the globe, you never know when necessity or opportunity may come calling.

CAREER SAVERS
The Art of Blending In
The Tactics of Relocation

The Art of Blending In

Xenophobes need not apply.

Adjusting to a new and different environment is challenging. If you've never lived and worked outside your home state or region, you may find other people's attitudes and ways of doing things confusing and disorienting at first. In foreign countries you risk learning first-hand the meaning of culture shock. A good rule of thumb to bring with you when you're away from home is that it's *you* who is the visitor or foreigner. The art of blending in is seeking common ground and learning to stand on it comfortably.

Moving Away from Home

Go west, young man.
—John Babsone Lane Soule (Horace Greeley, to whom this quote is commonly attributed, picked it up from an article in the *Terre Haute Express* and used it in a *New York Tribune* editorial)

The United States, Australia, and Brazil are the largest countries in the world in which nearly everyone speaks a common language. In the U.S., we take for granted that everyone from Florida to Alaska speaks English. This commonality of language, however, belies the many contrasts that exist between the various regions, urban and rural areas, and ethnic pockets that persist or spring up anew.

Pace, interpersonal relationships, and values vary widely. Differences that are barely noticed during vacations and business trips take on added significance when you must live and work among them. Relocating, for example, between northern and southern states or between major cities and rural areas may require major adjustments. Some people are able to blend into new environments quite smoothly, while others are as uncomfortable as ducks out of water.

Going Overseas

And I say that Your Highnesses ought not to consent that any foreigner does business or sets foot here...
—Christopher Columbus

A lot of U.S. companies are moving their facilities—and their jobs— abroad. GM is one of those that maintains facilities outside the U.S.

to control costs and exploit cheaper labor. NAFTA is only the latest excuse for companies to plant or expand on foreign soil. The multi-nationality of customers is the driving force: To sell computer chips, popcorn, and banking services to people who don't watch American TV, you need to know more about them than the exchange rate of their currency. And since more U.S. companies are marketing their products and services abroad, an understanding of different accents, languages, interests, and values is the only way to bridge the eco-culture gap.

Bob Rollo, a partner with R. Rollo Associates, a Los Angeles search firm specializing in financial services, says that in certain professions, such as banking, you should jump at the chance for an overseas assignment. Senior bankers need international experience and knowledge to enhance their marketability.

> That's one small step for man, one giant leap for
> mankind.
> —Neil Alden Armstrong

Happily, you need not journey to the moon for your career to be enriched by travel.

> "I definitely leapfrogged," says former social worker Jerome Madigan
> (Brigid McMenamin, *Forbes*, February 27, 1995). Madigan was referring to
> his experience of working with a United Nations group in Poland, and
> assignments for Price Waterhouse in the Ukraine and Uzbekistan. On his
> return to the U.S., he was appointed manager of Price Waterhouse's
> International Privatization Group in Washington, D.C. Robert Carter was
> a bank credit analyst in Houston. When he discovered that the Institute
> for International Education was recruiting for work in developing
> countries, he signed on. Carter was sent to Nepal, where he helped to
> start a new bank. Shortly after his return, Tenneco hired him to analyze
> opportunities (related to his experience in Nepal) in South America and
> the South Pole. Kevin Dodge, a Connecticut College economics major,
> spent time with Salomon Brothers in Germany. "I grew a lot," he says,
> attributing to this experience his being hired by Barclays de Zoete Wedd.

> The tough-minded ..respect difference. Their goal is a
> world made safe for difference...
> —Ruth Fulton Benedict

Gary M. Wederspahn, vice president of Prudential Relocation Intercultural Services in Boulder, Colorado, tells us that "Employers want international managers who accept and work well with people of other cultures" (*National Business Employment Weekly*, October 15, 1995). He quotes AT&T human resources director, Richard R. Bahner: "Technical skills are necessary but not sufficient for a successful international assignment. In today's increasingly global business environment, managers must be able to handle the cross-cultural human dimensions effectively."

> Wederspahn tells of an engineer assigned by a major petrochemical company in Saudi Arabia, and a financial investments broker sent to Japan. The engineer, who was devoutly religious, was deported after arriving in Jubai with (Christian) religious pamphlets in his baggage; the broker, whose behavior proved too aggressive for his Japanese counterpart, lasted only a little longer.

> I believe only in French culture, and regard everything else in Europe which calls itself a "culture" as a misunderstanding.
> —Friedrich Wilhelm Nietzsche

The Overseas Assignment Inventory (OAI) is an assessment tool used to measure 15 attributes considered relevant to the likelihood of working and adjusting to foreign environments. If you are considering working abroad, try these on for size:

1. Motivation: your reasons for being interested in a foreign assignment.
2. Expectations: your positive and negative expectations of living in a foreign country.
3. Open-mindedness: your receptiveness to other ideas and traditions.
4. Respect for the beliefs of others: your ability to accept other people's religions and beliefs without judgment.
5. Trust: your trust and faith in others.
6. Environmental tolerance: your adaptability to unfamiliar and uncomfortable conditions.
7. Personal control: the degree of your personal control.
8. Mental flexibility: your willingness and ability to consider new ideas and solutions.
9. Patience: your ability to keep your cool when faced with frustrating circumstances.

10. Social Adaptability: how well you adjust to unfamiliar social conditions.

11. Initiative: your willingness to take charge of challenging situations.

12. Risk-taking: your willingness to cope with change and take calculated risks.

13. Sense of humor: your ability to see humor in new and confused circumstances.

14. Interpersonal interest: your interest in dealing with people.

15. Spouse communication: the level of communication between you and significant others.

Ask a close friend or family member to review your self-assessment, especially if you're inexperienced at foreign travel or know little about your planned destination. Don't gloss over any potential problems or weaknesses; you're better off avoiding a bad match than getting into an unhappy (and unsuccessful) situation.

The Tactics of Relocation

> Job mobility is connected to job competence, and vice versa.
> —Harold S. Hook

Certain industry-related careers are tied to particular regions. Airline construction is focused in Seattle, cars are manufactured near Detroit, most major book publishing companies are located in the northeast, and the fashion industry is contained within the radius of a few blocks in mid-Manhattan. Military careers are often synonymous with frequent relocation, and real estate and insurance sales depend on local client bases. If you want to remain in or move to a specific state or city, review the job market in your profession.

Other considerations include cost and quality of living, and strong geographical ties and preferences. If you hate commuting, Los Angeles may not be your cup of tea; if you were born and bred in Chattanooga where your family and friends all live, think twice before moving to Chicago. But if you want to jump on the fast track, you won't be able to stay home on the farm.

Making the Move

> Push on—keep moving.
> —Thomas Morton

When your employer wants to send you to a different locale, you have a decision to make that can have an enormous influence on your (and your family's) life. If you're looking for a job, find out where the best growth opportunities are located. One option might be to look for a solid company whose home office location is attractive to you.

> You are your first product, so positioning yourself in the market as an individual is extremely important.
> —Portia Isaacson

College professors, engineers, factory workers, administrators, and executives must often move to where the jobs exist in order to remain employed. Many relocate by choice to take advantage of opportunities, although sometimes they are imposed upon by their employers to make the move.

> Once upon a time, the Ford Motor Company was manufacturing automobiles in Texas under the proud slogan, *Made in Texas by Texans.* That's when the future father of the Ford Mustang was learning to sell trucks in the southeast U.S. Having already refused a headquarters-based promotion, the young man was informed that his next check would be on his desk the following week—in Detroit. Reluctantly Lee Iococca made the move, Chrysler was on the road to resurrection, and the Texas slogan evaporated in Michigan's exhaust.

> True friendship's laws are by this rule express'd,
> Welcome the coming, speed the parting guest.
> —Alexander Pope

Companies and individuals have been known to "assign" annoying and troublesome people to far-off places to keep them out of trouble ..or just out of the way.

> In 1984, British Prime Minister Margaret Thatcher sent her son, Mark, abroad to spare her embarrassment and potential threat to her political career. During these years, according to the *Sunday Times of London,* Mark Thatcher made his initial fortune by using his family ties to swing a controversial Saudi Arabian arms purchase. Next he was a director of Emergency Networks, a company that allegedly withheld around $3 million in employee taxes without troubling to pay them to the

government. He faced trial in 1996 on these and charges that employee medical insurance premiums were also gobbled up by the company. His final known victim was the thriving Ameristar Fuels Corp., which filed for bankruptcy and was sold amid allegations of serious malpractice. No wonder Mrs. Thatcher encouraged her heir to relocate from her domain.

Not Making the Move

> I'm ten years burning down the road,
> Nowhere to run, ain't nowhere to go.
> —Bruce Springsteen

Refusing relocation may not cost you your job, but it can limit your potential in company. However, there are some very good reasons for turning down a move, and you need to be aware of what they are and how to handle them. The two most common arguments for not relocating are because you like it where you are, or because you don't want to go to a certain place. One way not to go is to evade the issue; another is to refuse.

> 'Tis distance lends enchantment to the view.
> —Thomas Campbell

Physical removal tends to limit your visibility. Even if you do a great job, being distanced from the home office makes it difficult for you to mingle and network as effectively as those who remain closer to the action. So if you must serve time out in the field, keep your lines of communication open, make a concentrated effort to keep in touch with key individuals, and try to work your way back as soon as possible.

Once you are removed from a major hub of activity, your options for finding a new job (should you be fired or desire to leave) may be limited. Research suggests that outside salespeople are among the first to be let go during cutbacks, while the most secure positions are those right under the cost-cutter's nose.

At one time, the college textbook division of Science Research Associates (SRA) was based in Palo Alto, California. When they were ordered by their parent company to move to corporate headquarters in Chicago, they lost all but six members off their office staff. Traditionally, SRA promoted from their field sales staff, who in turn were largely recruited from experienced competitors based in major university centers. During and after the Chicago move, however, the company had trouble filling many of its main office openings. Salesperson after salesperson said "no" to being relocated, preferring to stay where they were. When the company fell on hard times, floundered, and died, the salespeople were left high and dry; they remained in their locations of choice, but with limited job opportunities.

> It's not that I'm afraid to die. I just don't want to be there when it happens.
> —Woody Allen

Some ninety percent of Utah's college graduates choose to remain within the state for reasons of geography and religion. They have decided where they want to live even before they begin to pursue careers. Most of us, however, have less definite plans about where we expect to live and work. When the order—or suggestion—comes to pack our bags, we're not always ready to take preemptive action.

The best way to deal with most problems is to avoid them in the first place. If you see people (more or less like you) being asked to relocate, anticipate the possibility of it happening to you. If you don't want to be sent to far-away places, start campaigning for a more congenial locale right now. It's easier to ask for what you want than to refuse what you don't want after it has been proposed. If you want to stay where you are, make yourself so useful that they'll want to keep you there.

> Elaine's company had a history of hiring managers from successful field sales staff. She analyzed the records and found that certain locations (large cities) appeared to produce the quickest promotions. When the Boston territory opened, she let her boss know that she was ready, willing, and able to take it over. In fact, she was already familiar with the area and had developed an acquaintance with the New England sales manager. Everyone concerned was pleased with her preparation and enthusiasm, and she got the assignment.

> ..man has stopped moving, if ever he did move.
> —Pierre Teilhard de Chardin

When all else fails you can always say "no, thanks." However, this may limit your future with your employer. Find out how they have dealt with other refusenicks in the past, and how you are now viewed by your boss and other decision makers. It may be prudent to seek other opportunities just in case. Even if your reasons for refusing are accepted, nobody likes to be turned down, especially by their employees.

▼▼▼
CAREER BUSTER 20

POOR INTERVIEWS MAY
LEAVE YOU UNEMPLOYED

When you're unemployed, you have to work all the time.
—Terry Bradshaw

Note: Significant portions of this chapter were adapted from the author's earlier work, "The Technical Interview: What You Need to Know and Do to Win," in the book, *Ace the Technical Interview* (McGraw-Hill).

Interviews are a necessary part of earning a living for most of us. Fortunately, it is a skill at which you can probably improve, and it is likely to be worth your effort to do so. Consider this an investment not only in obtaining a job, but also in prospering and moving on to better jobs. The fundamental principles of successful interviewing, *preparation* and *presentation,* are the building blocks of nearly every facet of our professional careers.

Interviews are conducted to obtain information and evaluate people by the way they respond to questions. Interviewing skills are needed to create a positive impression, to present one's qualifications and assets in a favorable context, and to obtain information and commitments. Like most skills, interviewing techniques can be upgraded and refined through study and practice. You can improve your interviewing skills by reading up on what some of the experts say, and then practicing on some patient friends and family members. Interviewing is hard work, and getting yourself psyched up is an essential part of preparing to succeed. When you show up for an interview, always present the most confident and enthusiastic candidate you're capable of being.

CAREER SAVERS
The Art of Interviewing
Types of Interviews
Types of Interviewers
Interviewing Tactics

187

The Art of Interviewing

> Common sense is, of all kinds, the most uncommon.
> —Tryon Edwards

Preparation and presentation are the *yin* and *yang* of interviewing—its substance and its style. Interviewing has this in common with delivering a speech, making a presentation, and running a meeting: You must know what to say, and you must say it convincingly. The rest is about common sense, courtesy, and the same listening skills that serve us well in so many other areas.

When violations of common sense and courtesy occur during an interview they leave lasting impressions. An article in the *National Business Employment Weekly* (May 7-13, 1995), reprinted from the *Wall Street Journal,* revealed some amusing anecdotes collected from professional recruiters of career-destructive interviews. The men and women who committed them, including several senior executives, were guilty of amazingly poor judgment, ignorance, and rudeness. They were highlighted by a nail biter, a recent college graduate wearing a large nose ring, several who were more concerned with benefits, office furniture, and first-class travel than the particulars of the jobs for which they were interviewing, and one who actually put his feet on the desk of a female manager and instructed her to bring him a drink.

Types of Interviews
There are four major types of interviews that can influence your career: the *job interview,* the *status interview,* the *profile interview,* and the *termination interview.*

The Job Interview

> I am looking for an honest man.
> —Diogenes

> Interviewer: *Sorry, but I don't think we have enough work to keep you busy.*
> Interviewee: *It really doesn't take very much.*

Job interviews may be conducted formally in offices or in casual settings, such as over drinks, at dinner, or on the golf course. Whatever the locale, the interview is an evaluative process whereby the interviewer tries to verify your qualifications and desirability for a position. A good interview can enhance your chances of receiving an offer; a bad interview may eliminate you from further consideration.

The Status Interview

> If you work faithfully eight hours a day, you may
> eventually get promoted to a position where you work
> twelve hours a day.
> —Robert Frost

Status interviews, also called *reviews,* are conducted to evaluate an employee's performance. Your next raise, promotion, or assignment can depend on a positive status interview. It may determine whether you survive the cut during a staff reduction or a merger between departments.

Some status reviews are automatically scheduled at specified intervals, e.g., yearly, biannually, or three to six months after you begin a job. These are easy to prepare for since they are predictable. In most cases, your preparation is similar to getting ready for a job interview, except that you'll be talking about what you have accomplished where you are instead of somewhere else. The other important difference is that the person interviewing you is intimately acquainted with your track record, and you may need to respond convincingly to criticism. Otherwise the paths run parallel: Prepare for the interview, listen carefully to what is said, and present your accomplishments and goals in the best possible light.

The Profile Interview

> I do not mind lying, but I hate inaccuracy.
> —Samuel Butler

Profile interviews are the primary realm of journalists, writers, researchers, and those who wish to acquire information and personal opinions that they may or may not attribute to you. Whether you are famous or of lesser renown, people from within or outside your organization may desire to interview you for a variety of reasons. When this happens, ask the purpose of the interview and the context and medium in which your views may be recorded. For example, you may not wish to appear to take sides on a delicate company issue, or to be quoted in a certain journal. Bear very much in mind that the tone of your responses is likely to color the image in which you are cast; and the context should be clear and unambiguous to lessen the likelihood that you will be misquoted.

The Termination Interview.   Many companies use the termination
interview as part of their dismissal procedure. This is when the employee is commonly informed of the reasons for the termination and
of such details as payments due them, insurance options, and any ongoing responsibilities. If you've been fired, released, excessed, dis-
missed, discharged, axed, or let go by any other euphemism, this
may be your last chance to clarify:

1. what you might have done wrong, i.e., the official reason for your
   termination;
2. the amount of money due you, and the status of your retirement,
   insurance, and other benefits;
3. what may be required of you, including turning over accounts
   or information, returning certain records and equipment, and
   confidentiality.

Listen carefully and take notes on what is said. If any of these issues
is not covered, ask about them. However hurt or angry you may be,
keep your emotions under control. Don't try to talk them into letting
you keep your job because it's already gone. Above all, avoid arguing and saying or doing anything improper. Behaving with dignity
will give you the most satisfaction later on. Remember, too, that the
last impression you make on people will influence the way they talk
about you after you leave.

Types of Interviewers
Aside from placement agents and executive recruiters, there are two
major types of employment interviewers: screeners and deciders.

Screeners

> Speak the truth and shame the Devil.
> —François Rabelais

The screening interview is usually a formal, impersonal meeting conducted by a professional interviewer in the human resources department. Its purpose is to weed out the more obviously inappropriate
candidates by verifying their background, credentials, appearance,
and any overt characteristics. The screening interviewer may be
skilled at encouraging you to reveal facts you'd rather not discuss,
e.g., discrepancies between what you say and what is written on your

résumé, or why you left a certain company. Their purpose is to gather enough relevant information about you to enable them to make a safe decision as to whether to pass you on to the decision maker or the doorman.

In a very real sense, screeners are focused on uncovering reasons to stop you from getting any further. So it is more important that they don't find anything wrong with you than that they like you. Your objective in a screening interview is to pass. This means providing the screener with solid and consistant facts that fit into a wholesome picture. You need only satisfy the screener, not impress him. Respond clearly and fully to all questions while volunteering absolutely nothing. Avoid any hint of suspicion or controversy. If the screener is not impressed with you, you won't be able to charm or fast-talk your way past her; if she's satisfied with your credentials, the more you talk, the wider and deeper the potential pitfall.

Deciders

> Judge not according to the appearance.
> —*The Holy Bible*: John 7:24

The decision (hiring) interview is commonly conducted by a department head, manager, project leader, supervisor, or any combination thereof. Unlike the screener, the decision maker likely knows a good deal more about the job than about interviewing techniques. Decision makers are concerned with your ability to do the work and how you'll fit into the environment. And since they are going to interact with you on a daily basis, it matters that they feel comfortable with you.

The decision interview is where you must be prepared for job-related questions and informal conversations on a more personal level. You may have to convince potential supervisors and colleagues that you are, in addition to being competent, a reasonably agreeable person. You may use your interpersonal skills to direct the interview in a positive direction. And you'll want to get the information that helps you to make up your own mind about the job.

Agencies and Recruiters. Employment agencies and executive recruiters are screeners with a mission, for they earn their keep by placing candidates in salaried and consulting positions. Agency interviewers vary from knowledgable professionals to clerical note-takers; this often depends upon the level of the job to be filled and the amount of the commission. Recruiters tend to be sophisticated executive types, with the difference that they are also canny interviewers. If they think you're worth their client's time, they'll prep you thoroughly before sending you on an interview.

Interviewing Tactics

> Let each man exercise the art he knows.
> —Aristophanes

The tactics of successful interviewing consist of obtaining worthwhile interviews, preparing for them, and creating a positive impression during the interviews. Whether you are unemployed or exploring better options, there are a lot of people out there who are seeking the same opportunities. Strong interviewing skills can be your path through the crowd and into the winner's circle.

Getting Interviews

> Until opportunity knocks, look for doors to knock on.

Prior to preparing for an interview, you must first *get* the interview. This is generally accomplished through personal contacts, agencies, postings, advertisements, and self-marketing. Don't get discouraged if the interviews don't come fast and furiously at first, and never take the brush-offs personally. Most of the reasons potential interviews do not materialize have absolutely nothing to do with you, so keep your head and spirits up. Sometimes it's a numbers game: The more contacts you make, the more interviews you get, and the more likely you are to receive a job offer.

Employment agencies and recruiters maintain contacts with companies and organizations seeking staff. Recruiters generally specialize in upper-level positions, while employment agencies do most of their business on the entry, junior, and middle management levels. Both receive their fees from the employer, so their loyalties are naturally inclined in that direction.

Networking (Chapter 16) is still the major source of gaining interviews.

You can use the mail or telephone to promote yourself to prospective employers. Broadcast letters and phone calls are similar to cold sales calling, although the prospect may be warmed if you demonstrate knowledge of your target and their company. Networking tactics apply here as well.

When you respond to newspaper or journal ads, you become a very small fish in a large pond. If the advertiser is identified, do some research to distinguish your application; if the ad is anonymous, do what you can to make yourself stand out.

Preparation

> I'm turned off by people who haven't done their homework.
> —Donald Kendall (chairman of Pepsi-Co.)

The foundation of a successful interview is preparation (Chapter 21). As one human resources executive put it, "More candidates who don't get the job they want lose out because of a bad interview than a lack of qualifications. And most bad interviews are the direct result of a lack of preparation."

Your résumé is your emissary to everyone you'd like to meet. Think of it as the initial link in the job chain you wish to enter, the only voice that speaks for you until you have a chance to speak for yourself. Whether you go through an agency or contact a client directly, you need a current résumé to help you stand out among the hundreds, perhaps thousands of others who may be competing with you for the job. According to the *Résumé Handbook* (Arthur D. Rosenberg and David V. Hizer, Bob Adams, Inc., 3rd Edition, 1996), only one interview is granted for every 245 résumés received.

Orient your résumé specifically toward the position for which you are applying. It should include a summary of experience with at least two or three job-related accomplishments. Unless you are a consultant, your résumé should probably include a chronologically organized section (filling in any significant time gaps) to show growth, responsibility, and consistency. A consultant's résumé needs to display technical and related skills, experience, and clients.

Most résumés can be limited to two pages (one page for recent graduates and people with limited work experience); lists of publications, patents, and related credits may be attached. It helps to maintain your résumé on a word processor to keep it current and to quickly produce variations that emphasize specific skills and experience that may be of interest to a potential employer. Your résumé must be clearly organized and detailed without appearing cumbersome. It is often useful to have personal business cards, a telephone answering machine, and a fax machine.

▼▼▼

The first step in getting ready for an interview is preparing for the kinds of questions you are likely to be asked. Find out as much as you can from your contact or intermediary about specific job requirements, e.g., specific skills and administrative responsibilities. Related issues include location, hours, and opportunity for advancement. If technical knowledge is required, refresh your memory by referring to a book or notes. *Ask yourself what you would ask a candidate if you were conducting the interview, and be prepared to answer no less than that.*

Try also to find out who your interviewer is likely to be—a company executive, a department head, a project leader or manager, or someone from the personnel department. Is the interviewer a decision maker or a screener for someone else? If you are going to speak with a decision maker, be ready to meet some members of the team as well.

Just about any large company can be researched in the reference books available in most libraries. These include the *Standard & Poor's Records, Stock Reports,* and the *Register of Corporations, Directors and Executives; Moody's Industrial Manual;* and *Dun & Bradstreet's Million Dollar Directory* and *Middle Market Directory.* There are also directories of corporate affiliations and of foreign firms, and a wealth of other resources. Ask at your library if they subscribe to *Infotrac,* an online service providing research reports on literally thousands of companies. You may be able to obtain a company's annual report, and perhaps a copy of their house organ, by contacting or establishing an acquaintance within the organization.

If you're meeting an executive, they may be listed in one of the above references, in *Who's Who,* or in an online database of newspaper and newsmagazine articles and references. Get in touch with anyone you know in the company, or in a competing organization, and ask if they know the person you will be meeting. If you are unable to learn anything about the interviewer, observe carefully the office, desk, manner, and speech during the initial stages of the interview to pick up any clues as to interests and personality. If you discover a mutual interest or background (e.g., you attended the same college or worked for the same company), try to use it to establish rapport.

Everyone, from the naive beginner to the seasoned pro, needs to be mentally ready for an interview in order to be at their impressive best. When all other things are more or less equal, i.e., when two or more candidates are of comparable competence and experience, then confidence and enthusiasm for the job may serve as the tie-breaker.

Remember that the people who take the time to interview you have a need to fill, and it is to their interest to fill it as quickly as possible. This is a time-consuming task for the department head or manager who has the opening. Think of yourself as a potential solution to their problem.

Reliability. When you succeed in getting an interview, be punctual. Plan to arrive early enough so that unforseen delays won't make you late. Excuses for arriving late are still excuses, even if they're true. Being late is failing to arrive on time, and you don't want a potential employer's initial experience with you to be tainted by any kind of failure. If you are going to be unavoidably delayed, call the interviewer before the time of the scheduled interview to apologize for the inconvenience, and ask if it would be more convenient to delay the interview or reschedule it.

Objective. Just as the objective of a résumé is to get the interview, the objective of an interview is to convince the screener to pass you on to the decision maker, and then to get the job offer. This means convincing them that you not only have the right qualifications for the task, but that you have the right chemistry to fit into their culture.

When you go on an interview, always give it your best shot, with confidence and enthusiasm. Don't waste the interviewer's time—or your own—with an *I don't really want this job* attitude. And don't shoot yourself in the heel with a *You probably won't offer me the job* air, because if that's your attitude, they probably won't. The bottom line is winning the offer. You may later decide not to accept the job if you feel it isn't right for you, or if something better is available, but that decision lies in the future. At worst, if they do not offer you the job, you will have gained the experience of the interview for the investment of your time.

Presentation

You've got to talk the talk and walk the walk.

When a young job seeker was told that there wasn't anything available for him at Remington, he refused to give up. "I'm sure there is an opening for me," he insisted, "although I don't know where it is yet." He offered to work for a month without getting paid, betting his efforts against the chance of finding a job for himself somewhere in the

company. Sure enough, he was able to uncover several problems, and he
wrote up a proposal as to how he'd go about resolving them if given the
opportunity. And sure enough, Remington hired him.

If you're unemployed and think this approach is a waste of time and
energy, think again. On an average, it takes at least one month per
$10K of (last job) income to find a new position. Meanwhile, what
better way to invest your unproductive time? A company that agrees
to let you in the door—even without a salary—is likely to be impressed with your willingness to prove yourself. Even if you don't
land a job, you'll have an opportunity to make new contacts and
gain some valuable experience. Another plus is that while you're
working there, you can present yourself to other companies as being
on a consulting assignment (instead of unemployed).

If you are employed while seeking greener pastures, be prepared
for questions not only about the job for which you are applying, but
also about why you want to leave your current employer.

> Appearances often are deceiving.
> —Aesop

Personal appearance strongly influences the expectations of those
who meet us for the first time. Common sense dictates that the closer you conform to the norm (what you see around you), the more
you look the part. If you anticipate an extended interviewing process
that could last for several hours, wear clothing that will maintain its
neatness throughout the day.

Give references that will enhance your credibility toward the job
for which you are interviewing. Former employers, supervisors, and colleagues count for more than friends and family. Use academic recommendations if you are a recent graduate; but avoid using any references
with whom you have had no contact for a number of years without first
calling them. If you are uncertain of what someone may say about you,
check them out by having a friend call them as a potential employer.

Whenever people with different objectives get together, potential hazards come into play. A few of the more obvious examples include possible conflicts based on status and authority, gender, and
age. Differences of national origin, accent, and style are other factors
that can influence an interview.

The Interview: The Basics. Nobody wants to associate with a
grouch, especially another grouch. Interviewers are turned off by
complaining, bad-mouthing, arrogance, rudeness, exaggerated hu-

mility, and a general negative attitude or lack of enthusiasm. Conversely, a pleasant, upbeat, and courteous manner contributes to an atmosphere that is conducive to a successful interview. Greet the people you meet with a smile and a firm handshake. If you're kept waiting for a few minutes, a friendly chat with a receptionist or secretary may provide you with a valuable insight to use during the interview, e.g., "I appreciate your taking the time to meet me during your quarterly inventory," or "May I congratulate you on your recent award?"

> Early impressions are hard to eradicate from the mind.
> —Saint Jerome

Credibility is the most important impression to create during an interview. It is enhanced by appearing honest, confident, enthusiastic, courteous, and inoffensive. Speak in a manner that is natural for you; if you have memorized a bunch of technical details, deliver them in a conversational manner, not as if reading from a list. Avoid slang, sloppy English, profanity, and criticism (especially of a past employer or someone known to the interviewer); and do your best to avoid frequent use of "well," "umm," "y' know," and "like."

Set your mind on enjoying the interview; this can help you to relax and make a positive impression. Memorize the interviewer's name, and be sure to pronounce it correctly when addressing the person. Don't smoke, chew gum, or eat food or candy during an interview. It's okay to accept coffee, tea, or water if offered, although it may be safer to decline, especially if you're nervous. Remember that the interviewer is watching and evaluating your behavior.

Winners are those who can make quick adjustments to their environment. A successful interviewee pays attention to the interviewer and reacts accordingly. For example, suppose you are describing your last job and the interviewer's eyes begin to wander around the room: It's time to change the topic or ask a question. If the interviewer glances frequently at a clock or wristwatch, you are advised to keep your answers brief. When you do manage to catch the interviewer's interest, hold to that subject and to similar topics as long as may be reasonable.

Always listen carefully to what the interviewer says, whether it is what you want to hear or not. Skilled interviewers tell you precisely what they want you to know; unskilled interviewers may reveal more than they realize. In either case, the information they provide can help you to evaluate the interviewer, the company, and the job, and to respond in an appropriate and relevant manner. If the interviewer is terse, tense, or unpleasant, don't take it personally. He may be having a bad day, or perhaps that's just the way he is. Continue to conduct yourself with professional courtesy and enthusiasm, and hope for the best. Unless you experience this sort of unpleasantness often, chances are it isn't worth a second thought.

> It is not every question that deserves an answer.
> —Publilius Syrus

Answer questions clearly, accurately, and thoroughly without overexplaining or repeating yourself. Be consistent in your responses to different questions: This is most easily achieved by preparing some of your responses in advance, and by telling the truth. Most of the questions will address your qualifications and experience, your current or most recent position, and your reasons for wanting to join the company.

Be ready for the open-ended type of question, such as, "Tell me about yourself," or "What do you consider to be your major strengths and weaknesses?" In such cases, represent yourself in a believable and work-related manner, and discuss your assets objectively without overselling them. Above all, assume that if you are being truthful, you are being believed. With a skilled interviewer, the manner in which you respond to questions can be more important than the answers: Clear, decisive answers contribute to the image of intelligence and credibility.

> *Qualify.* Ask questions that help to define or clarify what is being asked of you. Example: "Are you more interested in how I designed the system, or in how I applied the methodology?" This keeps you from taking a false path and gives you a few extra moments to prepare your answer.
>
> *Clarify.* After answering a question, check the interviewer's demeanor. If she seems to be satisfied (e.g., she smiles or nods), pause to let her comment or ask another question. If she does not appear comfortable, ask if you have answered the question to her satisfaction and if there are any additional points she would like you to address.
>
> *Specify.* Tell what *you* did in your last job or assignment related to the position for which you are applying, aside from the team or group with which you worked.

Quantify. Describe your accomplishments in a meaningful context. Examples:

"I wrote over fifty programs averaging half a million lines of code in two years."

"We were the only group to complete our project on schedule."

"When my assignment was completed, I was assigned another task by the project leader."

Don't lie. Plausible exaggeration is the outer limit of creative expression when describing your experience and accomplishments. Employers tend to check up on their prospective employees thoroughly, and your reputation is your lifeline to success. Never lie to a potential employer—even the possibility of its discovery will haunt you.

Eye contact is the dominant feature in nonverbal communication. The way you meet or avoid someone's gaze can reveal volumes about your character and attitude. For example, looking away from the listener while speaking means *don't interrupt me even if I pause for a moment;* looking at the listener when you stop speaking is a signal that you're finished; and looking away from the person who is speaking suggests impatience or dissatisfaction with whatever is being said. [Chapter 2]

Always focus your attention on the interviewer rather than on the impression you are trying to make. Listen carefully to what he says and focus on his reactions to what you tell him. If he appears to lose interest, change course by asking a question:

"Have I answered the question to your satisfaction?"

"Was there something else you wanted me to address?"

"How many people are there in your department?"

"When do you plan to make a decision on this position?"

Before responding to a difficult question, pause just long enough to check your body language and compose your thoughts. If you get a question for which you are unprepared, tell what (if anything) you know, and admit your ignorance in a straightforward manner, e.g., "I have relatively little background in negotiating—is it essential to this position?" or "I would welcome the opportunity to sharpen my computer skills," or "I was not in-

formed that sales was a prerequisite for this position." Then try to
draw attention to an area in which you are more knowledgeable.

Many otherwise competent individuals have trouble fielding
some of the personal questions tossed at them in interviews. Be prepared for some or all of these questions:

Tell me about yourself.

What are your strong/weak points?

How do you feel about this or that?

Why did you leave your last job or want to leave your present
job?

Why do you want to join our company?

What do you want to be when you grow up?

Example 1:

Q: *Tell me about yourself.*

Prepare a two- to five-minute mini-profile in advance for this open-
ended query to avoid fumbling for words or revealing something
you'd prefer not to mention. Some of the topics you might use are
your ambitions, hobbies, leisure activities, and family, but this is
strictly up to you and what you're comfortable talking about.

A: *In my last two jobs my responsibilities were primarily research-ori-
ented. Although I'm pretty good with numbers, I was beginning to
feel isolated and would like to be more involved in customer relations.*

A: *I have a technical background, but I'm very interested in management. That's why I've been taking evening classes toward an MBA.*

Example 2:

Q: *Why did you leave your last job? (Why do you want to leave your
current job?)*

The majority of people who aren't terminated leave their jobs for better opportunities (money and prestige), because they're bored or dead-
ended, or due to a conflict with a boss or colleague. Responding to
this question is tricky because you don't want to be seen as complaining or criticizing.

A: *I've been purchasing automobile parts for over eight years, and I'm
ready to move ahead to the next stage of my career.*

A: *I was typecast as a creative type and I'm looking for a managerial
opportunity.*

A: *When they merged the two divisions, it was clear that there would be heavy cuts in marketing. Frankly, I'm a lot better at promoting products than at playing politics.*

If you were ousted because of a personality conflict that cannot be hidden, you may need to address it in a straightforward manner.

A: *When I transferred to the central region, I found that the regional manager had a very different set of priorities than my former boss and I. He was totally production-oriented, whereas I feel very strongly about quality. It was clear to both of us early on that we weren't comfortable working together.*

The Interview: Control

> Mankind will possess incalculable advantages and extraordinary control over human behavior when the scientific investigator will be able to subject his fellow man to the same external analysis he would employ for any natural object, and when the human mind will contemplate itself not from within but from without.
> —Ivan Petrovich Pavlov

Influencing the interviewer's perception of you, as we discussed earlier, depends on paying careful attention to what is said and done, perceiving what they appear to be looking for, and adjusting your approach accordingly. The closer you come to emphasizing those of your qualities that relate specifically to what the interviewer is looking for, the more successful you will be.

There are at least three good reasons to ask questions: first, to learn about the company; second, to show an interest in their accomplishments and goals; and third, to establish rapport with the interviewer. You can prepare a few perceptive questions in advance and compose additional queries during the interview.

One of the most successful strategies is getting the interviewer to do a share of the talking. *Note: This tactic is difficult to use on a professional interviewer.* Even if you don't get to make all the points you'd like to make, avoid the temptation to interrupt a chatty person. An interview that is dominated by the interviewer is likely to leave her with a comfortable feeling about you. When an interviewer shows a tendency to talk about the company or any other topic, let her do so with a minimum of distraction. If the opportunity presents itself, politely ask a few semi-personal questions like: "How long have you been working here, if you don't mind my asking?" or

"What do you especially like about the company?" You never know what might get someone going. Don't get too personal, avoid political and religious issues, and stay clear of references to any physical characteristics. Remember, small talk can be a double-edged sword.

Handling Pressure. Pressure interviews are unusual, but you should be prepared for them. Occasionally they result from an incompetent interviewer, but more often they are premeditated ploys to discover how you react to stress. The rule of thumb in any and every circumstance is courtesy, tact, and confidence. Don't blow your cool: Never let yourself be baited into rudeness, anger, impatience, or agreeing with a point of view with which you really disagree. You can acknowledge the interviewer's point without agreeing ("I understand your point."), and you can politely disagree ("Your point is well taken, although I find that ..").

Following Up. If your interview was arranged by an agency, call your contact no later than the afternoon following a morning interview, or the very next morning (unless they call you first). If the interview was arranged through an intermediary, contact that person as soon as possible—he or she may be able to obtain some valuable feedback. Unless the agency, recruiter, or other contact tells you not to write or call, feel free to write a follow-up letter to thank the interviewer for extending you time and interest, and to reiterate your interest (or lack of interest) in the job. Be sure to follow up with any information or materials that you promised to provide.

Negotiating. When you negotiate a salary or rate, you have to balance two opposing facts of life: The less you agree to, the less you will have to live with; and the more you demand, the more attractive the competition may appear. Do your best to find out the company's salary range for the job you want, and how much you can reasonably expect them to pay you. Then consider the least you are willing to accept. Now you're ready to negotiate.

Never bring up the question of salary yourself; and try to avoid revealing what you are currently earning. If an interviewer says it's necessary to know what you are earning in order to make you an offer, you can suggest a range that you know to be within the ballpark. If you commit to a specific amount, be prepared to stick to it; if you back down on something as important as this, your ability to make and maintain decisions will be questioned.

Managing Your Expectations

> If they don't offer you the job, you can always turn it
> down.
> —Yogi Berra

Try not to let any one position become so important that you will be
severely disappointed if it doesn't work out, or that you allow yourself to accept a lower salary or rate if they call you back to negotiate. Conversely, don't talk yourself into believing that you did a bad
job at the interview. After all, whether you get the job or not, it's
only a job.

CAREER BUSTER 21

IF YOU DON'T DO YOUR HOMEWORK, YOU MIGHT AS WELL STAY HOME

> If you don't do your homework, you won't make your
> free throws.
> —Larry Bird

Homework consists of planning and preparation—you plan your menu, and then you prepare the meal. Ironically, people often spend more time planning their vacations than important projects, or even their careers.

Planning is the development of a method or a strategy: the direction your new house will face, its number of rooms, and the height of the ceilings. Preparation is what you do in order to enact your plan: the ground you dig to lay the foundation for your home and the concrete you pour to support it. Planning is the choreography of our dreams, while preparation is the rehearsal and long hours of practice by which we may hope to achieve them.

Without preparation, plans are likely to remain ideas beyond achievement. It is said that Mark Twain used to prepare his "impromptu" speeches at least two weeks in advance. Likewise, unplanned and undisciplined preparation may amount to little more than wheel-spinning that gets you nowhere for all your efforts. Rose Fitzgerald Kennedy attributed the political successes of the Kennedy family not to money but to "...meticulous planning and organization." They planned their strategies, organized their resources, and laid the groundwork for every step forward.

CAREER SAVERS
The Tactics of Planning
The Art of Preparation

The Tactics of Planning

> It is better to have a bad plan than to have no plan at all.
> —Charles de Gaulle

Planning is a discipline at which most people improve with time and experience. Even poor plans can produce some benefit, if nothing more than learning to create a better plan next time around. A good plan can save you time and effort, maximize the efficiency and effect of your preparation, and contribute to a positive result.

Phases

> An idea isn't responsible for the people who believe in it.
> —Don Marquis

The planning process can be broken down into two discrete phases: the *mental* and the *physical*. The mental phase is the idea that we create within our minds, on paper, or in computerized simulations; the physical phase is the structure that we follow.

The mental phase, where plans are germinated and developed, is carried out by a select few who often count on others to transform their ideas into physical reality. The majority of us spend our careers implementing other people's agendas, as when we take employment in a company and work to bring about our employer's plans and policies. On the job, we have little to say about *what* we do and so we express our creativity in *how* we do it.

Getting Organized

> Don't agonize. Organize.
> —Florynce R. Kennedy

Performance and results are based on organizing tasks and resources efficiently, accurately, and in a timely manner. Since complex things are usually made up of simple things, most large or difficult projects need a well thought out and detailed plan. Organization applies to every level of productive work. Employers want well-organized managers who, in turn, prefer well-organized workers. The way you organize your day affects the quality and timeliness of all your projects and, inevitably, your career.

Psychologist Eric Fromm wrote that "True freedom is not the absence of structure—letting the employees go off and do whatever they want—but rather a clear structure that enables people to work within established boundaries in an autonomous and creative way." There is no single right way to organize a plan, although certain general guidelines are followed by most successful planners. Your use of them depends upon your needs, strengths, experience, and objectives. Both good and bad habits tend to propagate themselves and build momentum of their own. A well-organized campaign creates positive momentum, whereas poorly structured plans are likely to tip downward and run out of control. Organize your objective into simple, bite-sized tasks that can be clearly labeled, scheduled, and assigned. As each task is completed, you can then begin to knit them back into the whole of which they are a part.

Plan your work and work your plan.

A strategy may be as simple as always agreeing with your customers or as complex as a business plan. For our purposes, it is the way you map your plan and develop a mental image of a specific goal.

An effective strategy creates win-win situations, not win-lose. It identifies your reasons for pursuing an objective; key issues, concerns, and likely obstacles; the positions and agendas of the people you expect to deal with, and how they may coincide or conflict with your own; potential allies and opponents; and the differences between the methods you plan to use and the results you expect to achieve.

Computer scientist Alan Zakon advises us to "Think of the sequence. You create something. You grow it. Then you really tie it down tight, making it as efficient as possible. These are very different jobs."

Sequence isn't only the order in which you do something, but also the way that you conceive it. A plan starts off with an objective: what you wish to gain or accomplish, where you'd like to be, when you want to get there, and how to do it. Proper sequence is the order that enables you to accomplish your objective in the most efficient way. It's like using building blocks to erect a solid edifice: Certain ones are better suited for the bottom and others for the top, one step at a time. First you do your project plan, next your business plan, then your career plan, and finally your life plan.

Too many cooks spoil the brothel.
—Polly Adler

In team sports, the assignment and definition of roles is clearly on display for all to see. The same principle applies to any activity in which two or more people need to cooperate in order to get something done. If a single player doesn't know what is expected of him or her, the equilibrium of the entire team can be disrupted. Responsibilities must be defined at the beginning, before confusion, dissension, or negative momentum can set in. If someone is unhappy with his or her role, you need to come to terms with them by explaining, negotiating, redefining, or reassigning. And see to it that all your players understand each other's roles.

Don't get distracted by nonessentials. Stick to your plan or modify it, but don't allow yourself to be diverted from your purpose. Remember that the plan is not the objective, but a map to get you there; if the terrain changes along the way, you may need to modify the plan accordingly.

> Let's look at the record.
> —Alfred (Al) Emanuel Smith

The more complex your line of work, the more vital it is for you to maintain up-to-date records of essential information. Costs, milestones, problems, and accomplishments are among the items you may find it useful to record. This can help you to assess the validity of your original plan, to alter it as needed, and to better control the outcome.

Using Information

> Facts are stubborn things; and whatever may be our wishes, our inclinations, or the dictates of our passions, they cannot alter the state of facts and evidence.
> —John Adams (in 1770)

> Facts are stupid things.
> —Ronald Reagan (misquoting John Adams, in 1988)

Information science is the study of data: what it is, how it is collected, and the way it's used. Computerized storage and retrieval systems are used to handle large volumes of facts and figures. They can log, sort, and display information just about any way you want it. However, they can't determine *what* to store or *how to use it.*

> There is a profound difference between information and meaning.
> —Warren G. Bennis

Experienced businesses and individuals study the components and patterns that bear on their activities and apply the information to their plans. The trick to successful research is to know what you're looking for, where to find it, and how to store it. Once you have collected your information, it must be evaluated, organized, and applied in order for it to be of any use to you. Many organizations have acquired far more information than they know how to use. Often the data they so desperately need to solve their problems and make decisions is right under their noses, but no one has recognized and organized it into an accessible and usable format. Or it may be bottlenecked by a few people who either are too busy to make it readily available or use their control to further personal agendas.

> "We hired a CIO [Chief Information Officer] to decide what kinds of information to keep and how to store it," says the president of an Indiana farm supplies distributor. "The trouble is, nobody outside the information systems group knows enough about the system to use it independently, and we have to rely on them to get anything done."

> Outside of the killings, we have one of the lowest crime rates in the country.
> —(Washington D.C. mayor) Marion Barry (in 1989)

Even the most expert opinion must be subjected to cautious scrutiny, especially when it appears to contradict common sense. Vague and misleading phrases, numbers, statistics, flowcharts, and colorful graphical representations enable clever people to twist almost any fact into conformity with their own schemes.

> In Spain, the chairman of the state-run tobacco company declared that, according to unspecified scientific studies, "..moderate smoking is good for your health." (*Conde Naste Traveler*, August, 1995).

Forecasting

> Do not let your plans for a new world divert your energies from saving what is left of the old.
> —Winston Churchill

Forecasting is an attempt to predict events and trends. Over time, new patterns emerge and our plans need to take them into consideration. For example, power companies know when to expect peak demands on electricity and heating fuels, and retailers have a good idea when to stock up on swimsuits or ski equipment.

Successful forecasting requires a reasonably accurate vision of the future, an action plan to get you there, and contingency plans when things do not occur precisely as expected. "In complex situations," write Hillel J. Einhorn and Robin M. Hogarth of the University of Chicago Business School's Center for Decision Research, " we may rely too heavily on planning and forecasting and underestimate the importance of random factors in the environment. That reliance can lead to delusions of control." (*Harvard Business Review,* January, 1987)

> Wall Street indexes predicted nine out of the last five recessions.
> —Paul Samuelson

The "experts" differ in their abilities to predict future events and conditions. Stewart Alsop III believed he could "..perceive what the issues are before they become issues." Neils Bohr, however, quipped that "Prediction is very difficult, especially about the future." John Kenneth Galbraith summed it up this way: "There are two classes of people who tell what is going to happen in the future: those who don't know, and those who don't know they don't know."

This is not to suggest that we ignore the future, but that our forecasts be etched in flexibility rather than stone. Why do some investment fund managers have consistently better results than others? Because of their ability to evaluate and apply essentially the same information as their competitors. In any given period they may experience an occasional setback, but over the long haul they outperform the rest.

> Unpredictability cannot be removed, or perhaps even substantially reduced, by excessive planning.
> —Tom Peters

The best way to deal with the uncertainty factor is to plan for it. How? By building in contingency measures and fall-backs that can cut your losses and minimize the time and effort needed to make adjustments. According to Peter Drucker, "The only thing we know about the future is that it is going to be different."

> ..when you have eliminated the impossible, whatever remains, however improbable, must be the truth.
> —*Sherlock Holmes* (by Arthur Conan Doyle)

Laurel Cutler, vice chairman of FCB/Leber Katz Partners, insists that "There is no data on the future." However, there's no dearth of data on the past, where facts are unconfused with speculation. What has occurred is obvious in retrospect. History may be subject to interpretation, but it's still the clearest source of information available.

Planned Flexibility

> Any plan is bad which is not susceptible to change.
> —Bartolommeo de San Concordio

Robert Townsend (*Further Up the Organization*) recommends that organization charts be drawn up in pencil. "Never formalize, print, and circulate them," he cautions, or they may lose their flexibility.

> Whatever can go wrong will go wrong.
> —(attributed to) Captain Ed Murphy

These Murphy-like aphorisms combine a touch of humor with conventional wisdom:

- If more than one thing can go wrong, it will.
- If it's too good to be true, it probably isn't.
- When things are going better than expected, expect trouble.
- Whatever you think you know, knows things that you don't.
- The most critical detail is either missing or misstated.
- If you think things can't possibly get worse, they already are.

Athletes plan for competition and conditions. Top performers in every field walk mentally through each step in order to anticipate what will or will not work and the amount of time, effort, and resources they are likely to need. Of course, it is impossible to anticipate everything that could happen, but an awareness of the most likely possibilities can help prepare you for the unexpected.

Most of us make contingency plans every day without even thinking about them: We store a spare tire in the trunk of our car; we back up important computer files and documents; and we purchase insurance policies. The more crucial and vulnerable the objective, the more important it is to create a safety net around it. This may take the form of training additional staff to perform vital tasks in case a key team member is unable to perform, setting resources aside in case of need, or generally expecting anything that can go wrong to do so at the worst possible time. If you fail to build in enough redundancy to compensate for Murphy's laws, sooner or later you'll get hurt; if there's no Plan B, then one will probably be needed.

Overcoming Resistance

> (The death of democracy) ..will be a slow extinction from apathy, indifference, and undernourishment.
> —Robert Maynard Hutchins

There are people who have an aversion to the planning process: They create excuses, get sidetracked, or just don't make the effort needed to set themselves on track. This reluctance to do what's good for them may stem from a fear of commitment, naiveté, laziness, or some deep-seated desire to make things more difficult for themselves—as if life weren't difficult enough.

The way to overcome resistance to planning or any other necessary practice is similar to learning to take risks (Chapter 17): Think about what's needed to accomplish your objective. Start with simple, uncomplicated plans and work your way up; force yourself to make the effort in the beginning; and don't forget to reward yourself for making and sustaining the effort. Track your results—you're likely to discover that your planned activities turn out better than those that you've conducted by the seat of your trousers.

The Art of Preparation

> Being ready isn't enough. You have to be prepared ...
> —Sun Tzu

Now that you have your plan, you can prepare to implement it. Decide what needs to be done to enact the plan: research; gathering, modifying, and creating materials; selecting and training personnel. If you are working alone, find out what resources, help, and any special information or training you will need in order to enact your plan, and prepare yourself accordingly. If you're managing a project that will require additional staff, you'll need to select them, assign them to their specific duties, and provide for their training.

Preparation Based on Planning

> The future belongs to those who prepare for it.
> —Ralph Waldo Emerson

Preparation based on planning is the way you acquire, enhance, and organize the skills and resources needed to enact your plan. If the project calls for six people and two backups, focus on selecting, orienting, and training them; if certain materials are required, start obtaining them and preparing them to be used. If certain types of information are required, either research them yourself or assign another qualified person to do it. Match your preparation to the plan as closely as possible, or modify the plan accordingly.

Staff Selection

> The meeting of preparation with opportunity generates
> the offspring we call luck.
> —Anthony Robbins

In principle, you'd like to select the most qualified people for your project; but in the real world, you may get whoever happens to be available. This means that you will need to spend more time orienting and preparing them for their tasks. The way you deal with the attitudes, skills, and experience of your staff is an essential part of your preparation.

Practice

> The harder I practice, the luckier I get.
> —Gary Player

One of the surest ways to improve performance and ability is to practice. "New research," says Florida State University psychology professor Anders Ericsson, "shows that practicing can help us to perform much, much better because it actually improves the way we think." (*Bottom Line,* September 1, 1995).

Practice is a combination of recognition and repetition: learning better ways of doing things and creating effective patterns. Your practice habits need to balance challenge with reason: They should stretch your abilities to their limit, but not too far beyond. Easy tasks won't improve your performance and ability, and unreasonable goals are likely to frustrate and demoralize you. There is a saying, "If at first you don't succeed, try something harder," but again, be reasonable with yourself. The idea is to strengthen confidence, not whip it into submission. Develop a mental image of what you're trying to achieve, and measure your performance against this image. If your performance falls short, find out where and why, and work at improving it.

The first rule, clearly, is to persist.
—C. Northcote Parkinson

Persistence and dedication are among the most important attributes for success. The philosopher Plutarch wrote that "Perseverance is more prevailing than violence; and many things which cannot be overcome together yield themselves when taken little by little." As flowing water dulls the sharpest edges and wears away the hardest stone, tenacity can often overcome the most overwhelming obstacles.

Courage is the price that life exacts for granting peace.
—Amelia Earhart Putnam

The dedication needed to succeed in a competitive environment requires focus and persistence. If you are driven toward a single-minded goal, you've learned to shut out distraction and discouragement. You work at it until you get it right, and then you do it over again until you get it even better.

CAREER BUSTER 22

OVERCOMING SEXISM AND OTHER KINDS OF DISCRIMINATION IN THE WORKPLACE

Our nation has had a long and unfortunate history of sex discrimination ...
—(Justice) William Joseph Brennan, Jr.

Have you have ever been prohibited from acquiring something you wanted or going someplace you wanted to be? Try to imagine a lifetime of exclusion from such things and places.

This chapter is primarily oriented toward overcoming sexism in the workplace. To this end, we asked, researched, and summarized what a number of successful women had to say. Of course, the larger question of discrimination affects not only women but also racial minorities, people above a certain age, and physically challenged individuals, among others.

Some of the minority leaders with whom we spoke suggested that many of the attitudes and practices that pose barriers to women also affect these other groups. Betty Friedan could have been describing the plight of any minority when she wrote: "This uneasy sense of battles won, only to be fought over again, of battles that should have been won, according to all the rules, and yet are not, of battles that suddenly one does not really want to win, and the weariness of battle altogether..." And Earl Graves (publisher and editor of *Black Enterprise*) might have been talking about women, Asians, or Hispanics when he said: "Every day we [blacks] must work to break down the barriers of racism by showing that we can be the best whether we are making deals on Wall Street or delivering goods on Main Street."

CAREER SAVERS
The Art of Coping
The Tactics of Change

The Art of Coping

> We know of no culture that has said, articulately, that
> there is no difference between men and women except in
> the way they contribute to the creation of the next
> generation.
> —Margaret Mead

Opportunities are growing at an ever-increasing rate for women, and there is more awareness of the obstacles that daily confront women in the workplace. Judith H. Dobrzynski (*Business Week*, November 21, 1994) reports that 583 of the top 1,000 U.S. companies have one or more women directors (up from 11% in 1993). And according to the *Wall Street Journal*, the percentage of women enrolled in U.S. universities and colleges has increased by 3% (to 30%).

However, tradition and habit die slowly: With notable exceptions, women are still impeded from competing with men on an equal basis, and glass ceilings remain firmly in place in many of our corporations and other institutions. In the words of Laurence Peter, "Most hierarchies were established by men who now monopolize the upper levels, thus depriving women of their rightful share of opportunities for incompetence." Or, it may be added, for success.

Confronting the ignorance of sexism, raising consciousness of the unfair and unreasonable employment practices directed toward women, and changing prevailing habits and attitudes are the prime agendas of many women's groups. Breaking into the good-old-boy's clubs, finding appropriate career opportunities, being recognized for your achievements, and fending off sexist behavior are some of the challenges many women face on a daily basis.

Challenges

> I don't in a day at my desk ever think once about what
> my sex is. I'm thinking about my job.
> —(Clevelend Federal Reserve Bank CEO) Karen N. Horn

Anyone can have problems with a boss, colleague, or client. However, there are certain difficulties with which women are predominantly faced. Jane White (*A Few Good Women*) profiles the experiences of "eleven of America's most successful female executives." Her summary of their advice to women in the workforce focuses on dealing with the following issues:

- spotting a problematic boss (and trading him for a better one)
- reacting to men who don't acknowledge your ideas (but use them as their own)
- male subordinates who resent reporting to a woman
- male clients who won't take you seriously
- using authority words to demonstrate your competence even outside your area of authority (to skeptical males)
- male clients who'd like to mix business with pleasure (and still make the sale)
- sexist requests (like being asked to take notes when dealing with peers)

Special Challenges

> I believe that first and foremost I am an individual, just as much as you are.
> —Henrik Ibsen

Sonja Guidry, who emigrated to the United States from the Dominican Republic at the age of 12, is a Project Manager at the New York City Housing Authority and President of the Professional Organization of Hispanic Employees. She told us that, "If you are a minority woman—especially black or Hispanic—you have to perform better than your male or white female counterparts to be considered a good worker." Ms. Guidry believes that many Hispanic women begin with a cultural disadvantage. "We're taught to stay behind our men. Even if we don't always realize it, we have a tendency to put the man first and ourselves second. In the workplace, we need to overcome this attitude and recognize that we're just as capable as any man." She continued, "The mistake some women make is to overreact to some of the things men say. If you want to fit into a predominantly male (business) world, to be 'one of the guys,' you can't make a big deal about every little comment. Of course, you have to know where to draw the line, and there are things I won't put up with, but if you're overly sensitive you make the men uncomfortable and create a barrier between you and them." Her advice to a career-oriented Hispanic woman is first to ask yourself if this is what you really want, and if you're willing to make the necessary adjustment. "If you're going to compete with men on an equal basis, you may have to set aside some of your traditional values, like putting men ahead of yourself."

Rita Jeninsky, a pattern maker in New York's garment industry, is a member of the Jewish orthodoxy. "I don't run into any special problems related to my religion at work," she says, "although the number of religious holidays I have to take off can be a little difficult."

Hilda Rodgers is Executive Director of New York City's Manhattanville Community Center and president of the NYCHA Branch of the NAACP. Ms. Rodgers told us that African-American women have enjoyed preferential treatment over their male counterparts in the workplace because "..they may appear to be less threatening and their behavior is often interpreted differently." However, Ms. Rodgers also expressed concern that black women are "disproportionately penalized in the wake of mergers and downsizing activities, especially in the public sector." She added, "Lately, I have seen fewer examples of African-American women on the lower end managing to climb the ladder from clerical to professional positions than in the past," perhaps because of the economy or an influx of highly trained and educated people entering the marketplace. Ms. Rodgers' advice to African-American women is quite similar to that offered by most experienced women in the workplace: "Focus on your goals, maintain your self-confidence, and don't get discouraged by the obstacles you encounter."

Strategies

> It seems that woman has more likelihood of success the higher she pitches her sights.
> —Germaine Greer

Connie Glaser and Barbara Steinberg Smally (*Swim With the Dolphins*) summarize the opinions of "top female managers across the country" as to what it takes to succeed in corporate America. We believe that their advice applies equally to men.

- Know the company inside and out.
- Request feedback.
- Help your boss to meet his/her objectives.
- Let people know that you want to expand your responsibilities.
- Recognize and fill needs.
- Position yourself to be at the right place at the right time.
- Develop good interpersonal skills.
- Deliver outstanding work.
- Don't let yourself get too comfortable or complacent.
- Don't let yourself grow discouraged.
- Take credit for your achievements.
- Ask questions.

Bear in mind that no single tactic will guarantee you a successful career. Think of them rather as pieces of the puzzle you must solve to
get you where you want to be.

> ..the more threatening and irreducible reality appears,
> the more firmly and desperately must we believe.
> —Pierre Teilhard de Chardin

Recognition of a problem is the necessary first step in attempting to
resolve it. Denying its existence is more likely to intensify than eliminate the problem. Marilyn Loden and Judy Rosener (*Workforce
America!*) caution that women who deny or refuse to acknowledge
the existence of sex discrimination are guilty of collusion. They "...
shift the ..focus away from finding productive solutions to serious
problems by denying the very existence of the problem."

A study by psychologist Florence Geis, of the University of
Delaware, concluded that audiences of both men and women were
more prone to smile or nod with approval at men and to frown with
skepticism at women speakers (*Boston Globe,* March 12, 1990).
This negative conditioning, which reflects the traditional attitudes of
many parents and teachers, is not easily altered. Other studies suggest that some of the reasons for women's lack of advancement are
rooted in their own behavior, such as when they fail to take advantage of internal networking opportunities with other women or are
reticent to apply for sales positions because of their assumption that
sales requires an aggressive personality.

> It doesn't matter where you start as long as you have a
> road map and consider every work day as training along
> the way.
> —Deborah Steelmen (Associate Director, U.S. Office of
> Management and Budget)

Hard work may be its own reward, but by itself it isn't likely to get
you any more than an underpaid and undervalued job working for
someone who takes most of the credit for your labor. To be rewarded for your work you must be recognized for your accomplishments.
You also need to assure yourself of proper visibility. Successful
women (and men) managers advise that working long hours (rather
than more visible hours) is a tactical mistake. "If you start early and
leave early," cautions investment broker Marilyn B., "all they notice
is that you leave early. The guys who roll in anywhere between nine
and ten, or even later, and stay until six or seven in the evening, are
the ones who get the recognition for putting in the hours."

Thou wert my guide, philosopher, and friend.
—Alexander Pope

If we tallied up all the tips we've heard and read by successful women to other women, getting a mentor would be in first place.

Loraine Binion, a (minority) Corporate Audit Manager at Levi Strauss & Co., emphasizes the need for allies. Binion allied herself with some of the political heavyweights through networking and made a concentrated effort to find influential mentors. "If you can impress these people to speak well of you, there will be someone other than your boss who can say, 'I know the right person for this job' when a promotion opportunity comes up."

Melissa Cadet is another minority woman who takes mentoring seriously: "..that's why I founded the Sacramento (CA) chapter of the National Association for Female Executives ..I'm personally a mentor for about twenty of these women and I'm doing it because I didn't have one and could have used one through the years." (A Few Good Women)

Oh I get by with a little help from my friends.
—John Lennon and Paul McCartney

Networking (Chapter 16) is important to everyone who is pursuing a career. In an article by Andrea Gabor (New York Times, January 8, 1995), a group of women health care professionals in the Boston area provide a model of just how helpful an intelligent and well-organized networking campaign can be to your career.

In 1984, about a dozen women executives in the health care field, who had been meeting monthly for seven years, came to a collective realization. "We realized that we had started low, and were now among the senior management of our organizations," said (founding member) Elaine Ullian. "We were all working for new C.E.O.'s. We could be C.E.O.'s. But none of us was." She continued, "There were three or four search firms that recruited for these jobs, and they didn't even know we existed."

They resolved to get themselves noticed and devised a carefully planned, methodological drive. They worked their phones, contacted local politicians and headhunters, and held seminars on practical and useful subjects. Whenever an upper-level position opened or was about to open, the members would call acquaintances and former colleagues to recommend one another. And they networked throughout the state with women executives in other industries.

Their strategy began to pay off: In 1985, Linda Shyavitz was appointed chief executive at Sturdy Memorial Hospital in Attleboro. Two years later, Ms. Ullian became C.E.O. of Boston's Faulkner Hospital, and

Judith Kurland was named C.E.O. of Boston City Hospital and also Boston's Commissioner of Health and Hospitals (over a half-dozen established men). Other A Team members took charge of several community hospitals. By 1994, the list of successful members had grown to include Lucy Farmer, vice president of Mount Auburn Hospital; Sandra Fenwick, Network Development of Beth Israel Hospital; Judith Kurland, chief executive of Lifespan Communications; Dorothy Puhy, C.F.O. of Dana Farber Cancer Institute; Marva Serotkin, president and chief executive of Cura Visiting Nurse Association; and Elaine Ullian, chief executive of Boston University Medical Center. "We knew if we didn't initiate an organized approach, it would never happen," says Ms. Shyavitz.

> The most potent weapon in the hands of the oppressor is the mind of the oppressed.
> —Stephen Bantu Biku

Everybody gets discouraged at times; the trick is not to stay there. Once the initial disappointment, anger, and/or frustration of a negative situation has settled, you need to get yourself back on track to look for other opportunities. Discouragement is a disservice to yourself. Never mind how many reasons you can give for feeling bad—the bottom line is that you cannot afford to give in to them.

Opportunities

> There's always room at the top.
> —Daniel Webster

Given that the entire playing field is not yet equal, where do the best opportunities for women lie? In 1971, Ramona Arnett recommended, "If you're not a white male, consider sales seriously. Most employers, regardless of how sexist or racist they may be, will pay for any sales they can get." Richard Neblett, president of the National Action Committee for Minorities in Engineering, contends "...the line jobs are the ones that give you the training that you need."

> I am married to my business.
> —(American Toyota Dealership CEO) Betty Rivera

Sociologists Barbara Reskin and Patricia Roos (*Job Queues, Gender Queues*) identify eleven fields that used to be dominated by men that became "feminized" between 1970 and 1988. These include book editing, pharmacy, public relations, bank management, systems analysis, insurance sales, real estate sales, insurance adjusting and examining, bartending, baking, and typesetting and composition. During the same period, however, the status and earnings in these professions has diminished.

Sue Shellenbarger (*Wall Street Journal*, January 24, 1995) recommends sales as offering "...not only valuable experience on the fast track to management, but it leaves little room for discrimination..." However, Shellenbarger points to a two-year, nationwide study of 21 companies (by Catalyst) which revealed "potentially discriminatory screening tests, managers' negative stereotypes about women, women's lack of access to career-boosting mentors and networks, and difficulty entertaining customers in traditional ways such as fishing and golf outings." Catalyst also found that women comprise only 26% of the business-to-business sales force (whereas they constitute 46% of the entire work force); that only 14% of sales managers are women (mostly at the lower managerial levels); and that women in sales earn an average (mean) of 92 cents for every dollar earned by men—as opposed to a 70-cents-to-the-dollar gap in the workforce at large.

The computer industry offers technically able people a fast track regardless of their sex or ethnic origins. The demand for talented programmers and designers is established and growing. "If you can perform in this industry," says a high-level executive at a leading telecommunications company, "you're not black or white or male or female—you're solid gold." The world of finance is another venue open to results-oriented women like Apple VP and CFO Deborah A. Coleman. "I caught on to the finance stuff really fast," says Ms. Coleman. "There are things that you like to do, and then there are things that you are very good at. I would love to be a Broadway star, but I am not Bernadette Peters. I am very good at finance."

> Change the environment ...
> —Richard Buckminster Fuller

Many local, national, and international companies are making energetic efforts to provide a more hospitable environment for women. In addition, the number of women-owned and managed companies is growing at a healthy pace. A study by Dun & Bradstreet and the National Foundation of Women Business Owners shows that employment at women-owned companies in the U.S. grew between 1991 and 1994 by about 12%. These companies now employ some 15.5 million workers (more than the 500 largest companies), generate almost $1.4 trillion annually, and enjoy a 5% higher success-to-failure ratio over all U.S. companies combined. *Working Woman* magazine informs us that the nine largest woman-owned employers are Warnaco (N.Y.), Raley's (Sacramento), Little Caesar's (Detroit), Roll International (Los Angeles), Minyard Food Stores (Coppell, TX), Jenny Craig (Del Mar, CA), TLC Beatrice (N.Y.), Jockey International (La Jolla, CA), and Lillian Vernon (New Rochelle, N.Y.).

Some parts of the country may be more favorable than others for career-minded women. Ohio native Patricia Johnson (vice president of Blue Cross of California) believes that "California companies are very sensitive to diversity because our population is changing so rapidly before our very eyes: the mix of people, the color of people ..." (*A Few Good Women*). James Fallows (*More Like Us*) agrees that Californians are more optimistic about their opportunities. Other observers suggest that large cities and populations in flux offer more opportunity to women and minorities than those with a predominance of established companies and groups.

The wrong fight isn't worth the effort.

Everyone—men and women alike—needs to review their career objectives (Chapter 9) periodically, especially if they aren't enjoying their current activities. Unhappiness, frustration, or a lack of motivation may mean that you are doing something wrong, or that you're doing the wrong thing. If you get too caught up in the challenge of overcoming obstacles, you may lose track of what you really enjoy doing. Not everyone is cut out for corporate life in the fast track. In fact, many people find the atmosphere of smaller companies or entrepreneurial alternatives more satisfying and rewarding.

Moving Up

You can't hold a good person down.

The following are representative of the dozens of success stories that have recently come to our attention. (*Forbes*, March 13, 1995.)

> In 1980, Adelaide Horton joined the Chiat/Day advertising agency to install a new computer system. She rose to head of client accounting and financial director, left to join rival ad agency Lowe Group as chief operating officer, and then returned to Chiat/Day as chief operating officer. Following Omnicom Corporation's TBWA unit's purchase of Chiat/Day, Horton became chief operating officer of the combined $2 billion group.

When Susan O'Malley was in junior high school, she got a B+ on a paper she wrote on what she'd like to be when she grew up: the head of a professional sports team. O'Malley took a step toward realizing her dream in 1986, when she joined the professional basketball Washington Bullets as director of advertising. Working her way up the corporate ladder as marketing director and executive vice president, she was named president of the organization in 1991.

The Tactics of Change

> You are young, my son, and as the years go by, time will change and even reverse many of your present opinions.
> —Plato

Since sexism and other forms of discrimination are illegal in this country, some employers are reluctant to admit that they exist. Nevertheless (and perhaps for the same reason), ownership and upper management are growing increasingly concerned with creating at least the appearance of providing equal opportunity in their companies. Many decision makers are finally recognizing and reacting to injustices they can no longer, legally and morally, ignore.

Harassment

> My difficulties [in obtaining Senate nomination as Ambassador to Brazil] go back some years when Senator [Wayne] Morse [who opposed the nomination] was kicked in the head by a horse.
> —[Congresswoman and diplomat] Clare Boothe Luce

James Bernstein (*New York Newsday,* April 6, 1995) suggests that sexual harassment in the workplace is being taken a lot more seriously than just a few years ago. "The number of sexual harassment complaints filed with the U.S. Equal Employment Opportunity Commission," Bernstein reports, "has risen dramatically, to 14,420 last year from 5,623 in 1989." [A lot of women in sales-related fields say that they experience sexual harassment but hesitate to report such incidents because "dealing with difficult customers goes with the territory."]

There is disagreement as to whether this trend is the result of heightened awareness and sensitivity or a fear of potential lawsuits, but the result is that sexual jokes and innuendo are becoming less prevalent in the workplace. "...[I]t's not always important to differ-

entiate between the ethics and the finances," says Harry Van Buren
of the Interfaith Center for Corporate Responsibility. "Whatever
gets companies to do what they should do is what we're in favor of."

Attitudes

> I therefore claim to show, not how men think in myths,
> but how myths operate in men's minds without their
> being aware of the fact.
> —Claude Lévi-Strauss

Pamela Mendels (*New York Newsday,* April 23, 1995) reports that
executives with daughters entering the professional workplace are
more actively facing many of the issues confronting equal opportunities for women. "..[I]t is clear," says Mendels, "that in subtle ways,
daughters are exercising influence in the corporate suites occupied by
their fathers."

> J. Michael Cook, chairman and chief executive of Deloitte & Touche, has
> two career-oriented daughters: one a Wall Street trader, the other a
> marketing manager. He personally presided last year over a study leading
> to "a path-breaking initiative to topple barriers that have kept women
> out of the highest ranks of the accounting field." "I couldn't in good
> conscience be head of an organization that offered less to women than I
> would expect for my daughters," says Cook.

Mary Mattis of Catalyst (see *Action,* below) agrees. In a survey
of 22 CEO's of Fortune 1000 companies, Dr. Mattis found that
about half of them referred to their daughters as having influenced
their views concerning the leadership potential of women. The
prospect of their daughters having to face career discrimination
"made them stop and think."

> Daniel Shybunko, president of GSE Dynamics Inc., has three daughters
> and two sons. "I've learned it's not an equal world out there," Shybunko
> admits. "If you have three daughters and you see them want to go into
> the business world and the obstacles they face, you want to reach out to
> women in the business world."

An increasing number of executives, struck by the difficulties
that their daughters are encountering in the workplace, are making
an effort to see that such problems and obstacles are rooted out of
their own companies.

Richard Stolley, founder of *People* magazine and president of the advocacy group, Child Care Action Campaign, cites many of the (male) executives to whom he speaks as telling him, "I never realized this was so much of a problem until it happened to my own daughter."

Action

> The old order changeth, yielding place to new ...
> —Alfred, Lord Tennyson

Mary C. Mattis is Vice President, Research and Advisory Services, of Catalyst, a national not-for-profit women's research and advocacy group based in New York City (205 Park Avenue South, New York, NY 10003-1459; tel: 212-777-8900). Dr. Mattis explained to us that Catalyst's mission is to work with corporations and professional groups to help employers address women's workplace issues and to enable women to achieve their maximum potential in business and the professions.

Catalyst provides published broad-based (national) studies and internal (proprietary) organizational assessments for corporations and professional firms. Their research and advisory services staff analyzes workplace barriers and opportunities for women and helps companies and professional firms develop successful strategies to retain, develop, and advance women. Accordingly, Catalyst is a major source of statistics relating to women in the workforce.

INDEX

▼▼▼

About the Author

Art Rosenberg is a communications consultant with many years of career-building experience. Coauthor of the newly released *Manipulative Memos: Control Your Career through the Medium of the Memo*, he also coauthored *The Resume Handbook*, which has sold over 200,000 copies and is on "The National Business Employment Weekly's Bestsellers" list.